Que® Quick Reference Series

PC Tools® Quick Reference

George Sheldon

Que® Corporation
Carmel, Indiana

PC Tools Quick Reference.

Copyright ©1989 by Que Corporation.

Library of Congress Catalog Number: 89-62430

ISBN 0-88022-472-X

93 92 91 90   10 9 8 7 6

Interpretation of the printing code: the rightmost double-digit number is the year of the book's printing; the rightmost single-digit number is the number of the book's printing. For example, a printing code of 89-4 shows that the fourth printing of the book occurred in 1989.

This book is based on PC Tools Deluxe Version 5.5.

Que Quick Reference Series

The *Que Quick Reference Series* is a portable resource of essential microcomputer knowledge. Whether you are a new or experienced user, you can rely on the high-quality information contained in these convenient guides.

Drawing on the experience of many of Que's best-selling authors, the *Que Quick Reference Series* helps you easily access important program information.

Now it's easy to look up often-used commands and functions for 1-2-3, dBASE IV, WordPerfect 5, Microsoft Word 5, and MS-DOS, as well as programming information for C, Turbo Pascal, and QuickBASIC 4.

Use the *Que Quick Reference Series* as a compact alternative to confusing and complicated traditional documentation.

The *Que Quick Reference Series* includes these titles:

1-2-3 Quick Reference
1-2-3 Release 2.2 Quick Reference
1-2-3 Release 3 Quick Reference
Assembly Language Quick Reference
AutoCAD Quick Reference
C Quick Reference
dBASE IV Quick Reference
DOS and BIOS Functions Quick Reference
Excel Quick Reference
Hard Disk Quick Reference
MS-DOS Quick Reference
Microsoft Word 5 Quick Reference
Norton Utilities Quick Reference
PC Tools Quick Reference
QuickBASIC Quick Reference
Turbo Pascal Quick Reference
WordPerfect Quick Reference

Publishing Manager

Lloyd J. Short

Product Director

Karen A. Bluestein

Editors

Fran Blauw
Cheryl Robinson

Technical Edit by

Central Point Software, Inc.
William Coy Hatfield

Proofreader

Peter Tocco

Indexer

Sharon Hilgenberg

Trademark Acknowledgments

dBASE, dBASE III Plus, and dBASE IV are registered trademarks of Ashton-Tate Corporation.

Lotus 1-2-3 is a registered trademark of Lotus Development Corporation.

PC Tools Deluxe is a registered trademark of Central Point Software, Inc.

Table of Contents

Introduction

PC Tools Quick Reference not only includes the quick reference information you need to manage your computer's disk drives, but reviews the various commands, options, and applications available with PC Tools Deluxe. You learn to work with associated programs such as PC Tools Desktop, PC-Cache, PC Secure, and Compress.

Because it is a quick reference, this book is not intended to replace the extensive documentation included with PC Tools Deluxe. This book highlights the most frequently used information and reference material required to work quickly and efficiently with PC Tools Deluxe. For example, there are literally pages of information included in the documentation on how to do scientific formulas on the Desktop's Calculator. This Quick Reference does not repeat that extensive documentation. Instead, this book tells you how to start the calculator and to perform simple calculations.

PC Tools Quick Reference is divided into sections by tasks, applications, and topics. One section, for example, is called "System Info." Suppose that you need to know the number of serial ports attached to and recognized by your computer. You can find the information you need under the "System Info" section. This section, as well as the others in the book, contains the information you need to understand and run a command, and what the information displayed on your computer screen really means.

Now you can put essential information at your fingertips with *PC Tools Quick Reference*—and the entire Que Quick Reference series.

PC Tools Applications

PC Tools is a package of powerful programs that offers a complete set of utilities and a desktop organizer. You can operate these programs in TSR (terminate and stay resident) mode by loading them into your computer's memory, and by using a hotkey (pressing two keys). You even can switch to these programs as you work in an application.

Features of PC Tools include pull-down menus, mouse support, full-color windows, and movable and resizable windows.

The main sections of the package follow:

COMPRESS	Application that can significantly speed up hard disk performance
DESKTOP	Complete desktop organizer that offers nine applications: Notepads, Outlines, Databases, Appointment Scheduler, Telecommunications, Macro Editor, Clipboard, Calculators, and Utilities
MIRROR/ REBUILD	Program that helps recover accidental erasure or formatting of your hard disk
PC-CACHE	Program used to speed up disks
PC FORMAT	Replaces DOS FORMAT.COM file
PC SECURE	Program that adds high degree of security to your files
PC SHELL	Powerful utility program that provides easy maintenance of your DOS system

Practice the utilities within the PC Tools package on a spare floppy disk, because improper use of the utilities can result in unusable programs or a computer that will not start.

Hints for Using This Book

Because PC Tools Deluxe consists of many different applications all provided in one package, this Quick Reference includes a subhead under each boxed header referring you to a specific PC Tools application. The subhead tells you which program to run to achieve the desired result.

For example, you might see the word "PCSHELL" under a heading such as "Compare Files." This tells you that the commands you need to execute are located in the PC Shell program.

Conventions used in this book

As you read this book, keep the following conventions in mind:

Press **F10**. From the **O**ptions menu, select **S**ave Configuration.

To choose this command, press the boldfaced blue keys: **F10**, **O**, and **S**.

Use the down arrow key ($\downarrow$) to select an item.

This command moves the highlight to an option within a window, such as a file, command, or selection.

To select **O**K, press **Alt-O**.

This command selects the chosen options within a PC Tools Deluxe dialog box.

Click the desired option.

With this method, you select an item by positioning the mouse cursor on the desired option, and pressing the mouse button once (usually the left button).

Click-and-drag the highlight bar to the first file you want to select.

Position the mouse cursor on the highlight bar. Then, hold down the mouse button, slide your mouse until the highlight bar is in the desired position, and release the mouse button.

Other important keystroke commands you use when working in PC Tools follow:

> Press Tab to move to the next selection within a dialog box.

> Press Shift-Tab to move to the previous selection within a dialog box.

To carry out a command, type the boldfaced letter of the command. Alternatively, press Enter to carry out any highlighted command.

To cancel commands

You can cancel a command or dismiss a dialog box anywhere in PC Tools by pressing Esc or F3.

To use alternate keystrokes

One of the things you may find confusing when you first use PC Tools, is that often you can execute a command in more than one way. Although this book does not always present the shortest commands (those requiring the least amount of keystrokes), the commands always work, no matter where you happen to be in the program.

Suppose, for example, that you want to execute the Print command. You can

> Press F10. From the File menu, select Print.

> or

> Press Alt-F. Select Print.

> or

> Press P.

You can see that you have three different keystroke options available to Print. As you gain more experience with PC Tools, you will learn different keystroke combinations that enable you to work faster within the program.

PC Shell keyboard shortcuts

Following is a list of keyboard shortcuts available from within the PC Shell program:

Key(s)	*Description*
Alt-Space	Size/Move Window
Ctrl-A	Select drive A
Ctrl-B	Select drive B
Ctrl-C	Select drive C
Del	Two-list Display
F1	Help
F2	Help Index
F3	Exit PC Shell
F4	Reset selected files
F5	Directory Info
F6	File Display Options
F7	Active List Switch
F8	Directory List Argument
F9	File Select Argument
F10	Select Menu
Ins	One-list Display
Ctrl-Enter	Run
Shift-F9	DOS
Tab	Switch Windows

Using a Mouse with PC Tools

Although you do not need a mouse to use PC Tools Deluxe, full mouse support is available. Using a mouse with PC Tools Deluxe makes operating the program faster and easier.

With PC Tools Deluxe Version 5.5, you can use both mouse buttons. For all mouse commands, use the left button of your mouse if it has two buttons. Use the right button of your mouse to select files, unselect files, and scroll through the File or Tree List, as follows.

To select files

1. Press and hold the right mouse button, and position the highlight bar on the first file you want to select.

2. Press and hold the left mouse button. Drag the highlight bar over any other files you want to select.

Files are highlighted and numbered as you select them.

3. Release both mouse buttons after you select all the files you want.

To unselect files

1. Press the right mouse button and position the highlight bar on the first file you want to unselect.

2. Press and hold the left mouse button. Drag the highlight bar over any other files you want to unselect.

As each file is unselected, PC Tools Deluxe removes the highlight and number from the file name.

3. Release both mouse buttons after you unselect all desired files.

To scroll through the File or Tree List

1. Move the mouse to the window you want to scroll through.

2. Press the right mouse button and drag the mouse to the top or bottom of the display to scroll through it.

To access menus

Position the mouse cursor on the menu name, and click the left button. A pull-down menu appears and displays the various options available within the menu.

To select an option from a menu

1. Position the mouse cursor on the desired menu. Click and hold the left mouse button.

2. Drag the mouse, causing the highlighted selection bar to scroll through the options on the menu.

3. When you locate the desired option, release the mouse button.

or

1. Position the mouse cursor on the desired menu, and click.

2. Move the mouse cursor to the desired item in the menu, and click the left mouse button.

3. When the desired option is located, release the mouse button.

To select an option within a dialog box

Move the mouse cursor to the desired option, and click the left mouse button.

To perform key combinations with a mouse

Sometimes, you must use a key on the keyboard in combination with the mouse. Remember to *press and hold* the key on the keyboard *before* you press the mouse button. For example, to move files with the mouse, you must first press and hold Ctrl, then press and hold the left mouse button. The command does not work if you press Ctrl after you click the left mouse button.

Using PC Tools on a Network

You can use PC Shell on a Novell Netware or IBM Token-Ring Network system, although subtle changes occur. The drives accessible on the network display as an additional drive letter on the Drive Command Line, which is located under the horizontal menu bar.

The following commands are not available on a networked drive:

> Directory Maintenance Prune & Graft
> Directory Sort
> Disk Info
> Disk Map
> File Map
> Rename Volume
> Search Disk
> Undelete

Verify Disk
View/Edit Disk

If you attempt to select one of these commands on a networked drive, PC Tools displays a message box telling you the function is not available on a network.

To print a directory or file to a networked printer, press **Ctrl-Alt-PrtSc**.

PC TOOLS COMMAND REFERENCE

Following is an alphabetical listing of PC Tools Deluxe commands and the procedures required to achieve specific results.

Active List Switch

PCSHELL

Purpose

Switches between windows on a two-list display. Although PC Shell enables you to have more than one window open, only one window is active. The active window is easily identified by the double-line border. Any other window displayed on-screen has a single-line border.

To select the Active List Switch

Press **F10**. From the **O**ptions menu, select **A**ctive List Switch.

Alternatively, press **F7**.

To switch between the File list and the Tree list, press the **Tab** key.

─────────
To select the Active List Switch using a mouse

From the **Options** menu, click **Active List Switch**.

Alternatively, click the window you want to make
active.

Appointment Scheduler ═══

DESKTOP

─────────
Purpose

Creates, edits, and views daily or monthly appointments
and projects.

This electronic calendar within PC Tools Desktop
contains a regular calendar, a to-do list, and a scheduler.

─────────
Notes

When you run PC Tools Desktop as a memory resident
program, you can recall and view the Appointment
Scheduler easily. Generally, you can add, delete, or
change appointments, even if you are working in another
program. To help you spot potential conflicts in your
schedule, overlapping times appear highlighted in the
duration bar.

The Appointment Scheduler includes an alarm feature
that you can set. You can use and attach macros to the
alarm so that other programs can run, even if you are not
at your computer.

The Appointment Scheduler uses its own files, which
are created with a .TM extension. Files with these
extensions appear in the File Load dialog box after you
start the Appointment Scheduler.

Having multiple files with the .TM extension is
advantageous because it enables you to maintain
schedules for several people or for an office staff sharing
the same computer.

To start the Appointment Scheduler

1. From the Desktop menu, select Appointment Scheduler.

2. Press Tab to select a file with a .TM extension from the File Load dialog box.

The Appointment Scheduler screen appears and consists of the following items:

Horizontal Menu Bar	Located at top of screen. Contains names of pull-down menus.
Window Border	Displays active window with a double border. Use a mouse to move top border.
Monthly Calendar	Located in upper left of screen. Month-by-month calendar, with selected date highlighted. Highlighted date is day shown on Daily Scheduler. Calendar is perpetual, with no end date.
	Use the movement keys (up-, down-, right-, or left-arrow key) to select a date on the calendar. If you go past the first or last day of the month, the calendar moves to the next month. Press PgUp or PgDn (or click the arrows at the corners of the calendar box) to change months. Press Ctrl-PgUp or Ctrl-PgDn to change years. Press Home to return the current date.
Daily Scheduler	Located on right of screen. Daily time planner, with selected time highlighted.
	Use up- or down-arrow key to change the selected time. Press PgUp or PgDn (or click the arrows at the corners of the Daily Scheduler box) to scroll through the day's schedule. Press Home to select the earliest appointment

time; press **End** to select the last
appointment time. Press **Enter** to
make an appointment for the
highlighted time. If an existing
appointment is scheduled at the
selected time, press **Enter** to edit or
delete it. If a note is attached (a full
Notepad file) to the selected time,
press **F6** to pop up the attached
Notepad.

To-Do List   Located in lower left of screen, lists
important things to do. Items are
listed in order of priority. Up to 80
items can be placed on this list,
although only eight can be
displayed on-screen. Notes can be
attached to the to-do list.

Use the **up-** or **down-arrow** to
select an item on the list. Press
PgUp or **PgDn** (or click the arrows
at the corners of the Daily
Scheduler box) to scroll through
the list. Press **Home** to select the
earliest appointment time; press
End to select the latest
appointment time.

The to-do list is independent of,
and not attached to, the Monthly
Calendar and the Daily Scheduler.

Scroll Bars   Located on the edge of a window,
used with the mouse to move
through the display.

Message Bar   Located at bottom of screen,
contains messages to guide and
assist you as you work with the
Appointment Scheduler.

To move around in the Appointment Scheduler

1. Press **Tab** to move among the Monthly Calendar,
the Daily Scheduler, and the To-Do sections of the
Appointment Scheduler.

Alternatively, click the desired section if you are
using a mouse.

2. Press **F4** to position the calendar on the current
   date. Press **Home** to select the current date only if
   the Calendar section of the Appointment Scheduler
   is active.

The Appointment Scheduler always returns to the last
date used.

To make a new appointment

1. Select the Monthly Calendar by pressing **Tab**.

2. Use the movement keys to select the date of the
   appointment.

3. Press **Tab** to select the Daily Scheduler.

4. Press the **up-** or **down-arrow** key to change the
   selected time.

5. Press **F10**. From the Appointment menu, select the
   Make new appointment option.

6. Type the starting and ending dates, time, and note.
   Select when the appointment is, its duration, and
   whether you want an alarm. You also can attach a
   note.

7. Select **Make** to enter the appointment.

A musical note symbol appears to the left of the time
when you set an alarm. A repeating appointment appears
with a double note symbol. An N appears when you
attach a note to the appointment.

To delete an appointment

1. Highlight the appointment you want to delete on the
   Daily Scheduler. Press the **up-** or **down-arrow** key
   to change the selected time.

2. Press **F10**. From the Appointment menu, select
   Delete Appointment.

3. Select **OK** to confirm the deletion and to remove
   the appointment from the Daily Scheduler.

To change an appointment

1. Select an appointment on the Daily Scheduler by highlighting it. Press the up- or down-arrow key to change the selected time.

2. Press F10. From the Appointment menu, select Edit Appointment.

3. Type any desired changes in the appointment.

To find the next appointment

Press F10. From the Appointment menu, select Next Appointment.

Alternatively, press F4.

To find an appointment

1. Press F10. From the Appointment menu, select Find Appointment.

   Alternatively, press F5.

2. Type the text for the appointment.

3. Press Enter to begin searching for the appointment.

To find free time

1. Press F10. From the Appointment menu, select FInd Free Time.

   Alternatively, press F7.

2. Type the start time and the stop time.

3. Press Tab to select Any Day or Work Day.

4. Type the duration of the time desired.

5. Press Enter to find the free time.

To show time usage

1. Press F10. From the Appointment menu, select Show Time. Alternatively, press F8.

   The Show Time Usage command displays five days at a glance. Solid dots indicate appointments; shaded areas indicate free times; transparent dots indicate potential conflicts.

2. Press Esc to return to the main window of the
   Appointment Scheduler.

To attach notes

Press F10. From the Appointment menu, select Attach
Note. Alternatively, press F6.

To create a new to-do entry

1. Press F10. From the To-Do menu, select New
   To-Do Entry.

2. Type the text of the to-do entry.

3. Type the Start Date and End Date, and enter a
   priority number. The priority number positions the
   entry on the to-do list. Select Attach Note, if
   desired.

4. Select Make.

To delete a to-do entry

1. Select the to-do entry to be deleted.

2. Press Enter, and a dialog box appears.

3. Press Enter to select Delete.

To change appointment settings

1. Press F10. From the Controls menu, select
   Appointment Settings.

2. Select the desired settings in the Appointment
   Settings dialog box.

3. Select OK to accept the new settings.

To select holiday settings

1. Press F10. From the Controls menu, select Holiday
   Settings.

2. Select the desired holidays.

3. Select OK to add the selected holiday on your
   calendar.

To delete old entries

1. Press **F10**. From the Controls menu, select Delete Old Entries.

2. Type the cutoff date from which to delete old entries from the calendar.

3. Select Delete to remove the entries before the specified cutoff date.

To use the wide display

1. Press **F10**.

2. From the Controls menu, select Wide Display.

To load files

1. Press **F10**. From the File menu, select Load.

2. Select a file from the File Load dialog box.

To save files

1. Press **F10**. From the File menu, select Save.

2. Select Save.

To print

1. Press **F10**. From the File menu, select Print.

2. Select from the following:

Today	Prints today's schedule only
Week	Prints week's schedule
Month	Prints month's schedule.

3. Select Print to start the printing.

To use the autosave feature

1. Press **F10**. From the File menu, select Autosave.

2. Type a number for the amount of minutes you want to lapse between each autosave.

3. Press **Tab** to turn on the automatic save.

4. Select OK to set the automatic save.

This feature automatically saves your Appointment
Schedule files after a specified time.

To exit without saving

Press **F10**. From the **F**ile menu, select E**X**it Without
Saving.

This option does not save your changes made in the
Appointment Scheduler window.

Attribute Change

PCSHELL

Purpose

Views the attributes of a file, and makes changes to the
file attributes. Also changes the date and time stamped
on the file by DOS.

Notes

The following file attributes can be attached to, or
deleted from a file:

Hidden	Makes the file invisible during regular DOS directory command execution. (Each time you issue the DOS DIR command, the file does not appear.) PC Shell can see files that are assigned this attribute.
System	Causes the system file to be hidden after you execute the DOS DIR command.
Read Only	Protects the file so that you cannot make changes or deletions. You can read only a file assigned with this attribute.
Archive	Used by the DOS BACKUP and PC Tools PCBACKUP programs. Enables the programs to determine which files need to be backed up during the execution of the

program. When a change is made
to a file, DOS changes the setting
of the archive bit, which indicates
the file has changed and should be
backed up the next time the backup
program is run.

Do not change the attributes of system files or copy-
protected files. Doing so can prevent your computer or
programs from working properly.

To change the file attributes or date/time stamp

1. Press **Tab** to select the Tree List window. Select the
   directory containing the file or files for which you
   want to view the attributes or the date/time stamp
   by using the cursor keys to highlight the directory.

2. Press **Tab** to select the File List window that
   contains the file or files for which you want to
   change the attributes or date/time stamp.

3. Use the movement keys to highlight the file or files
   you want to change. Press **Enter** to select your
   choice.

4. Press **F10**. From the **F**ile menu, select **A**ttribute
   Change.

   The following information appears concerning the
   selected files:

   > H = hidden file
   > S = system file
   > R = read-only file
   > A = archive bit is set
   > Time/Date
   > Size

5. Press the movement keys to move within the
   Attribute Service dialog box.

   To make changes quickly to a list of files, make the
   change to the first file and press the **down arrow**.
   This technique enables you to change the attributes,
   time, or date of a list of files.

6. Select **H**idden file, **S**ystem file, **R**ead-only file, or
   Archive bit to turn on the attribute. Select from the

same options to turn off the attribute. By typing the letter, you toggle the attribute on and off.

7. Move to the **D**ate or **T**ime field and type the new date or time.

8. Select **U**pdate to save the changes to the disk, and return to the main PC Shell screen.

To change file attributes using a mouse

1. Select the file or files you want to compare.

2. From the **File** menu, select **Attribute**.

3. Click the attribute letter to toggle the attribute on and off.

4. Click **Update** to save the changes to the disk.

Calculators

DESKTOP

Purpose

Within PC Tools Desktop you have four calculators available—algebraic, financial, programmer's (hex), and scientific.

Notes

The keyboard commands available when you work with the calculator follow:

Press	*To*
+	Add
-	Subtract
* or X	Multiply
/	Divide
Enter	Total or equal
C	Clear
%	Calculate percentages

M then + or -	Add or subtract a number from memory
M + R	Recall a number from memory
M + C	Erase a number from memory
D then a number	Set the number of decimal places
,	Toggle the comma display

To use a calculator

Press **F10**. Select **C**alculators, and then choose the type of calculator you want to use.

To use the algebraic calculator

The Algebraic Calculator works like a regular calculator. Enter the first number, followed by the command. Next, enter the next number, followed by an equal sign.

For example, to perform the calculation 12 x 8:

1. Type **12**.

2. Press * (the operation).

3. Type **8**.

4. Press **Enter**.

The numbers appear in the calculator display and the tape. Although many numbers can be calculated at one time, only eight lines are displayed on the tape. Approximately 1,000 lines are available to add in the tape.

Use the financial calculator to do calculations pertaining to interest on IRAs, mortgage repayment, and computing depreciation. Use the programmer's calculator to express calculations in Hex, Octal, Binary, and Decimal code.

Clipboard

DESKTOP

Purpose

Enables you to copy and paste text from one DOS application to another. The Clipboard is a temporary storage area for your text. You can copy text from a spreadsheet, for example, and then paste that text into a report you are writing in your word processing program.

To use Clipboard

Load Desktop in the memory of your computer. The Desktop should run in TSR mode.

The Clipboard copies text only. It cannot copy graphics.

To mark a block of text

1. Move the cursor to the location where you want to begin marking text.

2. Press F10. From the Edit menu, select Mark block.

3. Use the movement keys to move to where you want to mark the text in Clipboard.

To unmark a block of text

Press F10. From the Edit menu, select Unmark block.

To copy and paste from the Clipboard using hotkeys

You also can copy to and paste from Clipboard by using the hotkeys without entering Clipboard. Use the movement keys to mark a block of text to be copied, and press Enter. To copy text to the Clipboard, press Ctrl-Del. To paste text from Clipboard, press Ctrl-Ins.

To copy text from the screen

1. Press the Ctrl-Space bar hotkey to go into the Desktop.

2. Press F10. From the Copy/Paste menu select Copy to Clipboard.

3. Use the movement keys to move the cursor to

where you want to start copying text into the
Clipboard.

4. Press **Enter**

5. Use the movement keys to mark a block of text to
copy into Clipboard.

6. Press **Enter** to copy the blocked text into
Clipboard.

To paste from Clipboard

Text placed in Clipboard remains there until you replace
it or until you exit the program.

1. Use the cursor keys to move to where you want to
paste the text from Clipboard.

2. Press the **Ctrl-Space bar** hotkey to go to the
Desktop.

3. Press **F10**. From the **C**opy/Paste menu, select **P**aste
from Clipboard.

To edit text on Clipboard

You can edit any text you copy to the Clipboard. After
the Clipboard window is open, you can use the
following commands, in addition to regular cursor-
movement keys: **E**rase, **M**ark, **U**nmark a block, **D**elete
all text, **I**nsert **F**ile, or **G**oto.

To erase a block of text

1. Move the cursor to the location where you want to
begin erasing text.

2. Press **F10**. From the **E**dit menu, select **M**ark block.

3. Move the cursor to where you want to mark the text
to erase from the Clipboard.

4. Press **F10**. From the **E**dit menu, select **E**rase block.

To delete all marked text

1. Press **F10**. From the **E**dit menu, select **D**elete All
Text.

2. Select **O**K to confirm that you want to delete all
text in the Clipboard.

To insert a file in Clipboard

1. Move the cursor to where you want to insert a file in Clipboard.

2. Press F10. From the Edit menu, select Insert file.

3. Select the file you want to insert from the File Load dialog box.

4. Press Alt-L to Load the selected file.

To use the Goto command

1. Press F10. From the Edit menu, select Goto.

2. Type the line number you want to go to.

3. Press Enter.

The Goto command enables you to move to a specified line in the Notepad.

To search Clipboard

The Find and Replace command always searches from the cursor forward in Clipboard. You cannot use this command to perform a global search.

To use the Find command

1. Press F10. From the Search menu, select Find.

2. Type the characters you want to search for in the Find dialog box.

3. Press Tab to select, if desired, one of the following:

Case Sensitive	If setting is on, the Clipboard finds exact matches only. If you search for *the* and turn on Case Sensitive, for example, Clipboard ignores the word *THE*.
Whole Words Only	If the setting is on, Clipboard searches for words only, not part of a word. If you search for *his*, for example, and turn

on Whole words only,
Clipboard ignores the word
history.

4. Press **Alt-F** to **F**ind the next occurrence of the
desired text.

To use the Replace command

1. Press **F10**. From the **S**earch menu, select **R**eplace.

2. Type the characters you want to search for in the
Find dialog box.

3. Type the replacement characters in the Find dialog
box.

4. Press **Tab** to select, if desired, one of the following:

> **R**eplace One Time
> Replace **A**ll
> **V**erify Before Replace
> **C**ase Sensitive
> **W**hole Words Only

After highlighting the desired selection, press **Enter**
to accept this Replace command.

5. Press **Alt-R** to **R**eplace.

═ **Command Bar** ═══════════

PCSHELL

Purpose

Provides quick access to commonly used commands.
Located at the bottom of the computer screen on the
middle line of the Main PC Shell screen.

To use the Command Bar

Press any of the following keys to execute the
corresponding command:

> **C**opy
> **M**ove
> Dele**T**e

Rename
View
HeXEdit
FInd
Print
Locate
FileEdit
Undelete
Zoom

Compare Disk

PCSHELL

Purpose

Determines whether two separate disks are identical.
This command is similar to the DOS DISKCOMP
command. Both the source and target disks must be
exactly the same. You cannot use this command to
compare a 5 1/4-inch disk to a 3 1/2-inch disk, or a
floppy disk to a hard disk.

To compare a disk

1. Press **F10**. From the **D**isk menu, select **CO**mpare.

2. Select the **S**ource and the **T**arget drives from the
   Disk Compare dialog box.

3. Insert the source disk into the correct drive.

4. Press **Enter** to continue.

5. Insert the target disk into the correct drive.

   Depending on your hardware configuration, you
   may be prompted in the Disk Compare Service
   dialog box when to insert the target disk. If so,
   select **C**ontinue to complete the copy process.

6. During the disk copy process, these letters may
   appear in the Disk Copy Service dialog box:

C	Comparing track
R	Reading track

When a dot appears in the track, that particular
track has been compared to the target disk.

7. Select EXit to return to the main PC Shell menu.

To compare a disk using a mouse

1. From the **Disk** menu, click **Compare Disk**.

2. Click the **Source** and the **Target** drives within the
   Disk Compare dialog box.

3. Click **Continue** to start comparing the disks.

4. If prompted, insert a target disk into the correct
   drive. Then click **Continue** to complete
   the process.

Compare File

PCSHELL

Purpose

Determines whether two separate files are identical. The
files can be located on the same disk, on different disks,
in different drives, or in any directory. The files can
have different file names or can have matching file
names. You also can compare several sets of files at one
time.

To compare files

1. Select the file or files to compare.

2. Press **F10**. From the **F**ile menu, select CO**m**pare.

3. Select the drive that holds the files you want to
   compare. Press **Enter** to **C**ontinue.

4. Select **M**atching Names or **D**ifferent Names. If you
   select **M**atching **N**ames, the files are compared. If
   you select **D**ifferent **N**ames, the File Compare
   Service dialog box appears.

5. Type the name and extension of the file to be
   compared. Press **Enter** to **C**ontinue, and the files
   are compared.

PC Tools informs you whether the compared files are different in the File Compare Service dialog box. The sector and the offset (the actual position within the sector) where the difference is displays. The ASCII value of the differences is also reported. Select Continue to proceed with the comparison after each difference is reported.

If you select more than one file, Compare continues with each file in turn. After the comparison process finishes, PC Shell returns to the main screen.

To compare files using a mouse

1. Select the file or files to compare.

2. From the **File** menu, click **Compare**.

3. Click the drive that holds the files you want compared.

4. Click **Matching Names** to compare the files or **Different Names** to display the File Compare Service dialog box.

5. Type the name and extension of the file you want to compare. Click **Continue**, and the files are compared.

Compress ================================

COMPRESS

Purpose

Optimizes the performance of your hard disk. When DOS saves your files to your disk, they are randomly placed. This application rearranges your disk, thus moving your files to a single location on the disk. Compress does not compress the files, but stores the files together on the disk.

Note

After you use Compress, a prompt appears asking whether you want to run Mirror. Always reboot your computer after running Compress.

To start Compress

At the DOS prompt, type

COMPRESS

Alternatively, press **F10**. From the Applications menu, select Compress Disk (if you are working in the main PC Shell screen, and have not loaded the PC Shell into memory).

To perform a disk analysis

Press **F10**. From the Analysis menu, select Disk Analysis.

The Disk Allocation Analysis dialog box provides information about your disk. Compress advises whether Compress is recommended.

To perform a file analysis

Press **F10**. From the Analysis menu, select File Analysis.

The File Allocation Analysis dialog box displays information about possible fragmentation of files on the disk.

To perform a surface analysis

Press **F10**. From the Analysis menu, select Surface Analysis.

The Surface Analysis option checks all clusters on your hard disk to make sure that they are usable by DOS.

To sort directories

Press **F10**. From the Sort menu, select the desired option. (This option defines the type of sort performed during the compression.)

To use the Select Compress technique

Press **F10**. From the Compress menu, choose one of the following:

Unfragment Only
Full Compression
Full Compression with Clear

Unfragment simply unfragments your files; Full
Compression unfragments all files and moves all free
space to the back of the disk; Full Compression with
Clear unfragments all files, moves all free space to the
back of the disk, and erases all data in unused sectors.

To set ordering options

1. Press F10. From the Compress menu, select
   Ordering Options.

2. Select from the following:

Standard	Places files as specifyied by Compress
DOS	Places all the files in regular DOS order
.COM & EXE	Moves all .EXE and .COM files to the front of the disk

To analyze disk organization

Press F10. From the Compress menu, select Analyze
Disk Organization.

Compress indicates whether Disk Compression is
recommended.

To begin Compress

1. Press F10. From the Compress menu, select Begin
   Compress.

2. Press Enter to select Continue and to begin
   Compress.

To print a report

1. Press F10. From the Compress menu, select Print
   Report.

2. Select Printer or Disk to choose where you want to
   send the report.

You must select this command before you can use Begin
Compress. This option generates a report called
COMPRESS.RPT which tells how long it took to run
the program, the options selected, and the number of
used, unused, and bad clusters on the disk.

Copy Disk

PCSHELL

Purpose

Copies standard DOS floppy disks. This command is
similar to the DOS DISKCOPY command. Both the
source and target disks must be exactly the same. You
cannot use this command to copy the data on a 5 1/4-
inch disk to a 3 1/2-inch disk.

Notes

The Copy Disk command formats the target disk as it
copies to it. The target disk does not have to be
preformatted.

Any data already saved on the target disk is lost during
the Copy Disk command. Be sure that the target disk
contains no data files before starting this command. Use
the Copy File command to copy files to the target disk
without destroying data files already saved on the disk.

To copy a disk

1. Press **F10**. From the **D**isk menu, select **C**opy.

2. Select the **S**ource and the **T**arget drives from the
   Disk Copy dialog box.

3. Insert the source disk into the correct drive.

4. Press **Enter** to **C**ontinue.

5. Insert the target disk into the correct drive. Make
   sure that the target disk is not copy-protected.

   Depending on your hardware configuration, you
   may be prompted in the Disk Copy Service dialog

box to insert the target disk. If so, select Continue to complete the copy process.

6. During the disk copy process, the following letters may appear in the Disk Copy Service dialog box:

F	Formatting track
R	Reading track
W	Writing track

When a dot appears in the track, that particular track has been successfully copied to the target disk. After the copy process finishes, you return to the main PC Shell menu.

To copy a disk using a mouse

1. From the Disk menu, click Copy Disk.

2. Click the Source and the Target drives within the Disk Copy dialog box.

3. Click Continue to start copying the disk.

4. If prompted, insert a target disk into the correct drive, and click Continue to complete copying.

Copy File

PCSHELL

Purpose

Copies one or many files. This command can copy files to the same drive but into another directory, to the same drive but with a different or new file name, or from one drive to another.

To copy files

1. Press Tab to select the Tree List window. Select the directory containing the file or files you want to copy from the Tree List window. Use the movement keys to highlight the directory.

2. Press Tab to select the File List window which contains the file or files you want to copy. (In DOS

commands, this is commonly referred to as
the source.)

3. Select the file you want to copy by using the
   movement keys to highlight the file name.
   Press **Enter** .

4. Press **F10** . From the **F** ile menu, select **C** opy.

   If you are using the Single List Display, go to
   Step 5.

   If you are using the Two List Display to copy, PC
   Shell displays a message asking whether you want
   the files copied to the second or other window. (In
   DOS commands, this is commonly referred to as
   the target.) If you do, select **Y** es. A dialog box
   appears, and the files are copied.

   If you do not want the files copied to the second
   window, select **N** o. Continue with Step 5.

5. Select the target drive in the File Copy box by
   pressing the **down arrow** . Press **Enter** to select
   C ontinue.

To copy files when the target drive contains subdirectories

Press **Tab** to select the Tree List Window. Select the
directory you want to contain the file or files in the Tree
List window.

If the target drive already contains files with the same
file names, you can do one of the following:

- Select **Replace All** to replace all files in the target
  directory with the same names as the copied files.

- Select **Replace File** to replace the current file in the
  target with the same name as the copied file.

- Select **Next File** to skip the current file and go to
  the next file.

- Select **Skip All** to skip all the files to be copied, and
  to return to the main PC Shell screen.

- Select **Exit** to return to the main PC Shell screen.

As a file is copied into the same subdirectory or onto the
same drive, a File Copy Service dialog box appears.

Type a new file name, then select C ontinue by pressing
Alt-C .

The files are copied to the new location (the target). You
return to the main PC Shell screen when the copy
process is complete.

To copy files using a mouse

1. Click anywhere within the Tree List window to
   select that window.

2. Click the directory containing the file or files you
   want to copy from the Tree List window.

3. Click anywhere within the File List window to
   select that window.

4. Select the files to copy (the source) by clicking
   them.

5. Move the mouse cursor onto one of the selected
   files. Click and drag the file name to the target
   directory in the Tree List window. A copy box
   appears and moves with the mouse cursor.

6. Release the mouse button to start the copying
   process.

Database

DESKTOP

Purpose

The PC Tools Desktop offers a powerful Database
program. Some of the features of the Database are
compatible with dBASE III files: the capability to use
customized display forms created in Notepad, and the
capability to perform automatic phone dialing. If you
use the Desktop as a memory resident program, you can
access the Database. You can then locate phone
numbers, client names and addresses, or any other
information you have stored in the Database.

Notes

As you work with PC Tools Database, remember these guidelines:

- You can have up to 15 windows open at one time, and accordingly, more than one Database open at one time.

- You can have a maximum of 3,500 records per database.

- You can have a maximum of 128 fields per record.

- A record can have up to 4,000 characters.

- Database ignores the memo field in dBASE III.

- Database uses the .DBF extension for files containing database information, which is compatible with dBASE III. Record files, identified with the extension .REC, are used by Database only to maintain information on how to display the database, and are not compatible with dBASE III. Form files, identified with .FOR extensions, are standard Notepad files.

Components of the database window

The database window contains these parts:

- The Horizontal Menu Bar contains names of available pull-down menus and on-line Help.

- The Window Border indicates active window with a double-line border and inactive window with a single line border.

- The Close Box is used with a mouse only to close windows.

- The Database Window displays one record at a time from the database file.

- The Title Bar displays the database file name.

- Record tells you which record is currently displayed.

  To display records, use the Records Scroll Bar, the F4 or F7 key, or the Goto Record command from the Search menu.

- The Records Scroll Bar is used with   mouse to scroll through and display records.

- The Status Line reports cursor position and the form file name associated with the database.

- The Tab Ruler shows tab settings.

- The Default Form Display shows the labels: NAME, PHONE, and ADDRESS, followed by a colon, then field data.

- Scroll Bars are used with a mouse to scroll through the current record.

- The Resize Box is used with a mouse to resize a window.

- The Message Bar contains messages to help guide you through your work in Database.

Database Fields

From the Desktop menu, select Database. The File Load dialog box appears. You can load an existing database, or you can create a new database.

If you want to create a new database, you must enter a file name with a .DBF file extension, and then select New from the File Load dialog box.

The Field Editor dialog box appears and offers these options:

- The **Field Name** text box enables you to assign a name to a field. You can use any alphabetic letter, the underscore character (_), and numbers (for example, **LAST_NAME2**). Field names can not exceed 10 characters, and must begin with a letter. Lowercase letters are converted to uppercase. Use the underscore character (_) to separate words. You cannot use spaces or blank field names.

- **Field Type** enables you to decide whether you want to enter character, date, numerical or logical data in a field.

  A character field consists of any letters (A-Z) or numbers (0-9) that are used for identification, special symbols (#, $, *, &), and the underscore character(_). A social security number field is a good example (**199-19-1999**).

A field must contain at least one character, and can contain up to 70 characters. If you copy records from dBASE III, any information longer than 70 characters per character field does not copy.

Numeric fields consist of any number or value used in mathematic computations (for example, the amount received in a check). Database also considers the decimal point (.), plus sign (+), and minus sign (-) associated with a number as part of a numeric field. The plus and minus signs are optional at the beginning of a number.

The actual position of the decimal place is fixed once it is set. The fixed decimal position means numeric fields appear in columns with decimal points aligned. Numeric fields can contain 19 characters. The default numeric field is 0.

PC Tools Desktop Database does not perform computations within the database, but you can store values in numeric fields for use in dBASE III.

Logical fields consist of a single character representing a true or false condition in a database. True is represented as T, t, Y or y. False is defined as F, f, N, or n.

Use a logical field to divide the contents of a database file into two groups: one for which the condition is true and another for which the condition is false. For example, a lawyer with a database of client billing records can use **T** in the logical field to indicate the client paid the invoice, and **F** to indicate the client has not yet paid the bill. The default logical field is F.

Date fields always contain eight characters that store numeric codes for the month, day, and year. The format is MM/DD/YY. Date fields always assume the 20th century. The default date field is 00/00/00.

Use Date fields only as dates in the data manipulation. PC Tools Database date field cannot be used in dBASE III formulas.

- The Size text box determines character length of any particular field. Determine the size of a text box by the longest item in the field. If the longest FIRST_NAME in your database has 15 characters, for example, specify the size of the FIRST_NAME field as 15, even though some of the first names are less than 15 letters.

The size limits of the fields vary depending on the type of field:

Character	70 characters (minimum of 1 character)
Logical	One character
Date	8 characters
Numeric	Up to 19 characters (the size is determined by defining the maximum number of digits allowed in the field, and then determining the total number of digits to appear to the right of the decimal point).

- The Decimal text box specifies how many decimal places are to the right of the decimal point in numeric fields. If you specify 2, for example, every numeric value has at least three decimal places: 12.00, 4.71, and 1.58.

- Field Number marks the current field. To move through the fields, select the Next and Previous buttons before closing the dialog box.

- The Add option adds current described field definition to the database. Automatically appends the new field if the field added was the last one in the database.

- Next selects the next field. Use this option to move through the fields.

- The Save option saves all added field definitions in the database and then closes the dialog box. The field definitions display in the default form. You must save the database structure before adding records to the database.

- The Delete option deletes selected field. Use Next and Previous to move through and select fields.

- Previous selects previous field. Use to move backward through the fields.

- The Cancel option cancels database creation. Returns you to the Desktop menu without saving your database. You also can click the close box or press Esc to cancel the database.

To create a new database

1. Select Database from the main PC Desktop screen.

2. Type the file name of the database and press Alt-N.

3. Type the field name in the Field Name text box in the Field Editor dialog box.

4. Select the type of field desired (Character, Numeric, Logical, or Date).

5. Select Add.

6. Repeat Steps 3, 4, and 5, adding additional fields as often as needed.

7. Select Save to save the new database file.

To create a new form

1. Press F10. From the Desktop menu, select Notepad.

2. Type the name of the new form.

   Be sure to name the new form with a .FOR extension. Use a name other than one you are using for the database.

3. Select the New command button.

4. Type your text using the Notepad functions.

   You must enclose all field names in brackets ([ ]). To insert a file called CITY in the form, for example, type [CITY].

5. Press F10. From the File menu, select Save to save the Notepad file.

To load forms

1. Press F10. From the File menu, select Load.

2. Select the form in the Load Form dialog box.

Forms must have file names with .FOR extensions.

3. Press **Alt-L** to load the form.

To print information from the database

1. Press **F10**. From the **F**ile menu, select **P**rint.

2. Select one of the following:

   - **Print Selected Records** prints previously selected records only.

   - **Print Current Record** prints the current record only.

   - **Print Field Names** prints the list of fields used in the database.

3. Select **P**rint by pressing **Alt-P**.

To add a new record

1. Press **F10**. From the **E**dit menu, select **A**dd New Record. Alternatively, press **F8**.

2. Move the cursor anywhere within the field, and type the new information.

Database is automatically in Replace mode. To switch to Insert mode, press **Ins**.

To edit existing records

1. Press **F10**. From the **E**dit menu, select **A**dd New Record. Alternatively, press **F8**.

2. Move the cursor anywhere within the record and type the new information.

To delete records

1. Display the record you want to mark for deletion.

2. Press **F10**. From the **E**dit menu, select **D**elete Record.

The **D**elete Record command only marks the record for deletion; it does not actually delete a record. Only when you run **P**ack Database is the record actually deleted.

A database must contain at least one record. If you attempt to delete the last record, a warning appears.

To restore deleted records

Press **F10**. From the Edit menu, select Undelete Records.

The Undelete Records command undeletes all records marked for deletion. You cannot select a single record for undeletion in Database. You also cannot undelete records after using the Pack Database option.

To pack records

Press **F10**. From the Edit menu, select Pack Database.

This command deletes all records you marked for deletion with the Delete Records command.

To hide records

1. Display the record you want to hide.

2. Press **F10**. From the Edit menu, select Hide current record.

Use this command if you do not need all records in the database. You may want to eliminate certain records from being printed, for example.

To select all records

Press **F10**. From the Edit menu, choose seLect all records.

Use this command to select all hidden records located within the database.

To edit field names

1. Press **F10**. From the Edit menu, select Edit Field Names.

2. Select any option in the Field Name Editor to change your fields.

3. Select Modify by pressing **Alt-M** to record the changes.

4. Press **Alt-S** to Save the edited changes.

To sort your database

1. Press **F10**. From the **E**dit menu, select **S**ort database.

2. Select from the Sort Field Select dialog box the fields you want to sort. Select **N**ext or **P**revious to choose another field.

3. Press **Alt-S** to select **S**ort on the chosen field.

To select records

1. Press **F10**. From the **E**dit menu, select **R**ecords.

2. Type the field name of the record you want in the Select Record dialog box.

3. Type the field criteria search string.

4. Press **Alt-S** to choose the **S**elect button.

To find text in all fields

The **F**ind Text in All Fields command searches for the specified text in all the fields.

1. Press **F10**. From the **S**earch menu, select **F**ind Text in All Fields.

2. Type the text you want to find.

3. Select one of the following:

   - **Search All Records**
   - **Search Selected Records**
   - **Search from Current Record**

4. Press **Alt-S** to select **S**earch.

To find text in the sort field

1. Press **F10**. From the **S**earch menu, select Find **T**ext in the sort field.

2. Type the text you want to find in the sort field.

3. Select one of the following:

- **Search All Records**
- **Search Selected Records**
- **Search from Current Record**

    4. Press **Alt-S** to select **Search**.

Note that Find **T**ext in the Sort Field searches for text in the specified field only.

To go to a record

    1. Press **F10**. From the **S**earch menu, select **G**o to record.

    2. Type the number of the record you want in the Goto Record dialog box.

    3. Press **Alt-G** to select **G**oto.

To set document controls

To set the page layout

    1. Press **F10**. From the **C**ontrols menu, select **P**age Layout.

    2. Set the margins, paper size, line spacing, and starting page number.

    3. Select **O**K by pressing **Alt-O**.

To configure autodial

    1. Press **F10**. From the **C**ontrols menu, select **C**onfigure autodial.

    2. Set the dial to either tone or pulse, the printer communication ports, and the baud rate desired as based on your equipment.

    3. Select **O**K by pressing **Alt-O**.

To use Autodial

To use Autodial, you must have a Hayes-compatible modem attached to your computer.

    1. Display the record containing the phone number to dial.

    2. Press **F10**. From the **C**ontrols menu, select **A**utodial.

3. Pick up the telephone.

4. Press **Esc** to disconnect the modem. (Wait until the phone begins to ring before you press **Esc**.)

To save the document controls settings

Press **F10**. From the **C**ontrols menu, select **S**ave setup.

Date/Time

PCSHELL

Purpose

Sets the date and time on your computer's clock. This command performs the same function as the DOS DATE and DOS TIME commands.

To set the date or time

1. Press **F10**. From the **O**ptions menu, select Dat**E**/Time.

2. Type the new date in the Set Date and Time dialog box. You must enter the date in the MM-DD-YY format. Press **Enter** to accept the new date and to move to the time option.

3. Type the new time. You must enter the time in the HH-MM format.

4. Select **C**ontinue. The new time and date are set, and you return to the main PC Shell screen.

To set the Date/Time using a mouse

1. From the **Options** menu, click **Date/Time**.

2. Type the new date, press **Enter**, and type the new time.

3. Click **Continue** to return to the main PC Shell screen.

Delete

Purpose

Deletes or erases a file or multiple files. Similar to the DOS DEL command, the PC Shell Delete commands also can erase files assigned with the attributes Hidden, Read-only, or System.

To delete a file

1. Select the file or files you want to delete by using the cursor keys to highlight the file name. Press **Enter** to select the file.

2. Press **F10**. From the **F**ile menu, select **D**elete.

3. The File Delete Service dialog box displays the current file name and extension. Choose one of these four options:

   • Select **D**elete by pressing **Enter** to delete the file.

   • Select **N**ext File to skip the currently selected file, and to display the next file.

   • Select **D**elete All to delete all selected files.

   • Select **C**ancel to stop deleting files, and to return to the main PC Shell screen.

If you select only one file to delete, the only options available within the File Delete Service dialog box are **D**elete and **C**ancel.

To delete a file using a mouse

1. Select the files you want to delete by clicking them.

2. From the **File** menu, click **Delete**.

3. Click **Delete**, **Next File**, **Delete All**, or **Cancel**.

Desktop

DESKTOP

Purpose

The Desktop is a complete organizer that offers the following nine applications:

Notepads
Outlines
Databases
Appointment Scheduler
Telecommunications
Macro Editor
Clip**B**oard
Calculators
Utilities

Each of these applications is described in more detail in specific sections of this book.

Notes

If your system has enough memory, you can load Desktop into your computer's memory and run it as memory resident. To load Desktop as memory resident, at the DOS prompt type

DESKTOP /R

You also can press the **Ctrl-Space bar** hotkey sequence to load Desktop.

Press **Esc** or **F3** to cancel a message or dialog box in Desktop.

To start Desktop

To start Desktop at the DOS prompt, type

DESKTOP

and press **Enter**.

Directory Maintenance

Purpose

Adds a new directory, renames or deletes a subdirectory, changes to a current subdirectory, and prunes or grafts a subdirectory.

Pruning a directory means to move it from one subdirectory to another. *Grafting* means attaching a subdirectory from one subdirectory to another. When you prune and graft a directory, the entire directory, including its files, is removed from the first sub-directory, moved, and attached to its new position.

Notes

The Directory Maintenance command is similar to the DOS CD, MD and RD commands. However this command performs these commands in one operation, saving time, and eliminating frustrating typing mistakes.

Although the Directory Maintenance program is a quick, convenient method of changing and moving subdirectories, you must be careful when pruning or grafting (moving and deleting) subdirectories. Some of your programs may require a specific named subdirectory, and if you move or change it, your program may no longer work.

If you use the Directory Maintenance program to make changes to your directories, you may need to edit your AUTOEXEC.BAT file to update the path statement. You may also need to edit any other batch files used to start your programs.

If you are using PC Shell as memory resident, make certain that no files in the subdirectories to be changed are already in use by another program.

To add a subdirectory

1. Select the disk where the subdirectory is to be added. Press **Ctrl-A**, **Ctrl-B**, or **Ctrl-C** to select drive A, B, or C.

2. Press **F10**. From the Disk menu, select Directory Maint.

3. Select **Add a sub directory** from the pop-up menu.

4. If the selected drive contains subdirectories, the Subdirectory Add dialog box appears. Select a subdirectory where you want to add the new subdirectory by pressing the **up-** or **down-arrow** key. Then select Continue in the Sub Directory Add dialog box.

5. Type the name of the new directory (and extension, if desired) in the Sub Directory Add dialog box.

6. Select Continue to add the new directory.

To add a subdirectory using a mouse

1. Select the drive holding the disk where the directory is to be added by clicking the drive letters in the upper-left corner of the main PC Shell screen.

2. From the Disk menu, click **Directory Maintenance**.

3. From the pop-up menu, click **Add a Sub Directory**.

4. If the selected drive contains subdirectories, the Sub Directory Add dialog box appears. Click the subdirectory where you want to add the new subdirectory. Then click **Continue** in the Sub Directory Add dialog box.

5. Type the name of the new directory (and extension, if desired) in the Sub Directory Add dialog box.

6. Click **Continue** to add the new directory.

To rename a subdirectory

1. Select the disk where the subdirectory is to be renamed. Press **Ctrl-A**, **Ctrl-B**, or **Ctrl-C** to select drive A, B, or C.

2. Press **F10**. From the Disk menu, select Directory Maintenance.

3. From the pop-up menu, select **Rename a Sub Directory**.

4. Select the subdirectory you want to rename by pressing the **up-** or **down-arrow** key.

Note: The Root Directory on your disk cannot be renamed.

5. Select Continue in the Sub Directory Rename dialog box.

6. Type the new name of the directory (and extension, if desired) in the Sub Directory Rename dialog box.

7. Select Continue to rename the new directory.

If the new name you typed in the Sub Directory Rename dialog box is already in use, the new name is not accepted. You are returned to the Sub Directory Rename dialog box to type another name.

To rename a subdirectory using a mouse

1. Select the drive holding the disk where the directory is to be added by clicking the drive letters in the upper-left corner of the main PC Shell screen.

2. From the **Disk** menu, click **Directory Maintenance**.

3. Click **Rename a Sub Directory** from the pop-up menu.

4. Click the subdirectory you want to rename. Then click **Continue** in the Sub Directory Rename dialog box.

5. Type the name of the new directory (and extension, if desired) in the Sub Directory Rename dialog box.

6. Click **Continue** to rename the new directory.

To delete a subdirectory

1. Select the disk where the subdirectory is to be deleted. Press **Ctrl-A**, **Ctrl-B**, or **Ctrl-C** to select drive A, B, or C.

2. Press **F10**. From the Disk menu, select Directory Maint.

3. Select **Delete a subdirectory** from the pop-up menu.

4. Select the subdirectory you want to delete by pressing the **up-** or **down-arrow** key.

5. Select Continue in the Sub Directory Rename dialog box.

   Note: The Root Directory on your disk cannot be deleted.

6. Select Continue to delete the selected directory.

7. Select Continue again to confirm that the selected directory is to be deleted.

A directory must be empty before you can delete it. To remove files in a directory, use the Move Files command or the Delete Files command.

To delete a subdirectory using a mouse

1. Select the drive holding the disk where the directory is to be added by clicking the drive letters in the upper-left corner of the main PC Shell screen.

2. From the **Disk** menu, click **Directory Maintenance**.

3. Click **Delete a Sub Directory** from the pop-up menu.

4. Click the subdirectory you want to delete.

5. Click **Continue** in the Sub Directory Delete dialog box.

6. Click **Continue** to confirm the deletion of the directory.

To change the DOS current directory

1. Press **F10**. From the Disk menu, select Directory Maint.

2. Select **Change DOS Current** from the pop-up menu.

3. Select the subdirectory you want to make current by using the movement keys.

4. Select Continue in the Sub Directory Change dialog box to make the selected directory current.

To change the DOS current subdirectory using a mouse

1. From the **Disk** menu, click **Directory Maintenance**.

2. Click **Change DOS Current** from the pop-up menu.

3. Click the subdirectory you want to make current.

4. Click **Continue** in the Sub Directory Change dialog box.

To prune and graft a subdirectory

1. Select the disk where the subdirectory is to be pruned. Press **Ctrl-A**, **Ctrl-B**, or **Ctrl-C** to select drive A, B, or C.

2. Press **F10**. From the **D**isk menu, select Directory Maint.

3. Select **Prune and Graft** from the pop-up menu.

4. Select the subdirectory you want to prune by pressing the **up-** or **down-arrow** key.

5. Select Continue in the Sub Directory Prune and Graft dialog box.

   PC Shell marks the subdirectory to be pruned with the > symbol.

6. Select the subdirectory you want to graft (or attach) to the selected subdirectory by pressing the **up-** or **down-arrow** key. Select Continue to delete the selected directory.

7. Select Continue again to confirm that the selected directory (the directory marked with the >) is to be grafted to the highlighted subdirectory.

The Root Directory on your disk cannot be pruned.

To prune and graft a subdirectory using a mouse

1. Select the drive holding the disk where the directory is to be pruned by clicking the drive letters in the upper-left corner of the main PC Shell screen.

2. From the **Disk** menu, click **Directory Maintenance**.

3. Click **Prune and Graft** from the pop-up menu.

4. Click the subdirectory you want to prune.

5. Click **Continue** in the Sub Directory Prune and Graft dialog box.

   PC Shell marks the subdirectory to be pruned with the > symbol.

6. Click the subdirectory to which you want to graft (or attach) the selected subdirectory.

7. Click **Continue** to graft the selected directory.

8. Click **Continue** again to confirm that the selected directory (the one marked with the >) is to be grafted to the highlighted subdirectory.

To modify the attributes of a directory

1. Select the disk where the subdirectory is located that will have its attributes modified. Press **Ctrl-A**, **Ctrl-B**, or **Ctrl-C** to select drive A, B, or C.

2. Press **F10**. From the **D**isk menu, Select Directory Maint.

3. Select **M**odify Attributes from the pop-up menu.

4. Select the subdirectory you want to rename by pressing **up-** or **down arrow**. Then select **Continue** in the Sub Directory Modify Attributes dialog box.

5. Select **H**idden, **R**ead Only, **S**ystem, or **A**rchive in the Modify Directory Attributes dialog box.

6. Select **Update** to modify the new directory.

To modify the attributes of a subdirectory using a mouse

1. Select the drive holding the disk where the directory is to be added by pointing and clicking the mouse on the drive letters in the upper-left corner of the main PC Shell screen.

2. From the **Disk** menu, click **Directory Maint**

3. Click **Modify Attributes** from the pop-up menu.

4. Click the subdirectory you want to modify. Then click **Continue** in the Modify Directory Attributes dialog box.

5. Select **Hidden**, **Read Only**, **System**, or **Archive** in the Modify Directory Attributes dialog box.

6. Click **Update** to modify the new directory.

Directory Sort

PCSHELL

Purpose

Sorts the files in a selected directory. The files within a directory can be sorted by name, extension, size, date/time, or selected number. The files can be sorted in ascending order (from A to Z) or descending order (from Z to A).

You can view the list of sorted files and update the list after the files have been sorted. If you sort and update a directory, for example, the next time you perform the DOS DIR command, the files in the list are displayed in sorted order.

To sort a directory

1. Select the drive that contains the subdirectory you want to sort. Press **Ctrl-A, Ctrl-B**, or **Ctrl-C** to select drive A, B, or C.

2. Select the directory containing the file or files you want to sort in the Tree List window by using the movement keys to highlight the directory.

3. Press **F10**. From the **S**pecial menu, select **D**irectory Sort.

4. Select one of the following sorts:

   1 By Name   Sorts by file name

   2 By Extension   Sorts by file extension

3 By Size	Sorts by number of bytes in file
4 By Date/Time	Sorts by file date and time
5 By Selected Number	Sorts by number associated with selected files

5. Choose the **6** Ascending or **7** Descending sort method.

6. Press **Enter** to select Sort.

7. Press **Enter** to View the new sort order.

8. Press any key to return to the Directory Sort Service dialog box.

9. Select **U**pdate by pressing **Alt-U** to save the sort order, and to return to the main PC Shell screen.

To sort a directory using a mouse

1. Click the drive that contains the subdirectory you want to sort.

2. Click the directory containing the file or files you want to sort in the Tree List window.

3. From the **Special** menu, click **Directory Sort**.

4. Click one of the following sorts: **By Name, By Extension, By Size, By Date/Time,** or **By Selected Number.**

5. Click **Ascending** or **Descending** to select the sort method.

6. Click **Sort**.

7. Click **View** to see the new sort order.

8. Click once to return to the Directory Sort Service dialog box.

9. Click **Update** to save the sort order, and to return to the main PC Shell screen.

Disk Info

PCSHELL

Purpose

Provides additional, helpful information about a disk:
amount of available disk space, number of hidden files,
number of user files, and number of bytes located in a
bad sector.

To obtain disk information

1. Select the disk containing the information you
   want. Press **Ctrl-A**, **Ctrl-B**, or **Ctrl-C** to select
   drive A, B, or C.

2. Press **F10**. From the Disk menu, select Disk Info.

3. After you review the Disk Information dialog box,
   press **Enter** to Exit.

To obtain disk information using a mouse

1. Select the disk containing the information you want
   by clicking the drive letters in the upper-left corner
   of the main PC Shell screen.

2. From the **Disk** menu, click **Disk Info**.

3. Click **Exit** after you review the Disk Information
   dialog box.

Disk Map

PCSHELL

Purpose

Displays the sectors or clusters on a disk that are used by
files, as well as those sectors that are free or available
for use. In the Disk Mapping Service dialog box, each
position on the grid represents one cluster. Without
exception, DOS allocates one cluster at a time—not
sectors—on a disk for a file. However, clusters can be
different sizes, depending on the disk you are using.

Notes

With Disk Map, you can determine whether your files are fragmented (composed of sectors scattered throughout the disk). If your files are fragmented, you do not obtain maximum performance from your computer.

Each space on the grid, which represents one cluster, displays one of these symbols:

[ ] Available   Cluster is available for file storage.

B Boot record   Cluster contains disk's boot record. Every disk includes a boot record, even if it is not a DOS system disk (one that can start your computer).

F File Alloc Table   Cluster contains File Allocation Table (FAT). DOS uses FAT to keep track of location of files. FAT tells DOS where files are stored on disk and which clusters are still available.

D Directory   Cluster is disk's directory.

. Allocated   Cluster is part of a file.

h Hidden   Cluster is part of a hidden file.

r Read Only   Cluster is part of a Read-Only file.

x Bad Cluster   DOS has marked this cluster as bad and has made it unusable.

The Disk Map command is similar to the File Map command. Disk Map enables you to see all files on the disk in the map; File Map enables you to see selected files in the map on-screen.

To use Disk Map

1. Select the disk to be mapped. Press **Ctrl-A**, **Ctrl-B**, or **Ctrl-C** to select drive A, B, or C.

2. Press **F10**. From the **S**pecial menu, select Disk **M**ap.

3. Press **Enter** to return to the main PC Shell screen.

To use Disk Map with a mouse

1. Select the disk to be mapped by clicking the drive letters in the upper-left corner of the main PC Shell screen.

2. From the **Special** menu, click **Disk Map**.

3. Click **Exit** to return to the main PC Shell screen.

DOS

PCSHELL

Purpose

Leaves the PC Shell and enters DOS commands at the DOS prompt. You can reenter PC Shell at any time by typing **EXIT** at any DOS prompt.

Notes

PC Shell automatically frees up most of its memory requirements while at the DOS prompt, enabling you to run larger applications. However, some applications may not run because of insufficient memory when PC Shell is still RAM resident.

The DOS command is available only when PC Shell is in nonresident (Shell) mode. If you installed PC Shell as resident, you cannot access this command. In the File menu displays the word unavailable if you loaded PC Shell as resident.

To run the DOS command

1. Press **F10**. From the **Fi**le menu, select DOS.

Alternatively, press **Shift-F9**.

2. Enter any DOS command at the DOS prompt.

3. Type **EXIT** to return to the PC Shell.

To run the DOS command using a mouse

1. From the **File** menu, click **DOS**.

2. Enter any DOS command at the DOS prompt.

3. Type **EXIT** to return to the PC Shell.

Exit PC Shell

PCSHELL

Purpose

Quits the PC Shell Program and returns to the DOS prompt.

To exit the PC Shell program

1. Press **F10**. From the File menu, select EXit PC Shell. Alternatively, press **F3**.

2. Press **Enter** to exit.

To exit the PC Shell program using a mouse

1. From the **File** menu, click **Exit PC Shell**.

2. Click **Exit** to leave the program.

File Display Options

PCSHELL

Purpose

Sets how files are displayed and sorted in the File List window. The files are listed alphabetically according to file names.

You can choose to display the files with any of the following options:

Size	Displays file size
Date	Displays file date
Time	Displays file time
Attribute	Displays file attributes
Cluster Number	Displays file starting cluster number

You can select which of these options you want to display in the File List window.

The Current Display Options are listed on the top right of the screen.

Each time File Display Options sorts, you can choose whether you want the sort to be ascending or descending.

Choose a File Sort Order from this list:

Name	Sorts files by name
Ext	Sorts files by extension
Size	Sorts files by size
Date/Time	Sorts files by date and time
Ascending	Sorts files by selected options in ascending order
Descending	Sorts files by selected options in descending order
No Sort	Does not sort files. Lists files in the order they are placed in the directory (default setting).

The current sort order appears on the lower right of the screen.

To change the file display options

1. Press **Tab** to select the File List window.

2. Press **F10**. From the **O**ptions menu, select File Display Options.

    Alternatively, press **F6**.

3. Select any of the Display Options or the File Sort Options in the Set File Display Options dialog box.

4. Select **O**K by pressing **Alt-O** to change the File Display options and to return to the main PC Shell menu.

Use the **S**ave Configuration command from the **O**ptions menu to save your new settings for the File List window.

To use file display options using a mouse

1. Select the File List window by clicking anywhere in it.

2. From the **O**ptions menu, click **File Display Options**.

3. Click any of the Display Options or the File Sort Options in the Set File Display Options dialog box.

4. Click **O**K to change the File Display options and to return to the main PC Shell menu.

File Edit

PCSHELL

Purpose

Edits and creates documents when you work in the PC Shell. Not as powerful as Notepad, but can handle minor word processing needs.

File Edit commands

The following keyboard commands are available when you work in File Edit:

Key	*Function*
Any character	Inserts character at cursor
Space bar	Inserts space at cursor

Tab	Inserts tab at cursor
Enter	Inserts paragraph at cursor
Del	Deletes character under cursor
Backspace	Erases character left of cursor
Up arrow	Moves cursor up one line
Down arrow	Moves cursor down one line
Left arrow	Moves cursor left one character
Right arrow	Moves cursor right one character
Ctrl-left arrow or **Home**	Moves to beginning of line
Ctrl-right arrow or **End**	Moves to end of line
Ctrl-Home	Moves to beginning of file
Ctrl-End	Moves to end of file
Home (pressed twice)	Moves to beginning of window
End (pressed twice)	Moves to end of window
PgUp	Scrolls text up one window
PgDn	Scrolls text down one window

To access File Edit

1. Press **Tab** to select the Tree List window. Select the directory containing the file or files you want to edit in the Tree List window. Use the movement keys to highlight the desired directory.

2. Press **Tab** to select the File List window. Select the file you want to edit by using the movement keys.

   A dialog box appears asking whether you want to create or edit a file when you select **W**ord Processor.

3. Press **F10**. Select **F**ile menu, and File **E**dit.

4. Type text as desired.

Use the commands located at the bottom of the screen when you are in File Edit to perform various tasks. You can use these commands to Save, Search, Replace, Select, Cut, Copy, Paste, Show, and Exit.

File List Filter

PCSHELL

Purpose

Limits the files displayed in the File List window.

You can display only files in the subdirectory with the extension .EXE, for example, with this command. You can use the standard DOS wild card characters, * and ?, to list files with common file names, extensions, or characters. By typing ***.EXE** in the Dir List Argument dialog box, you display only those files with the .EXE extension.

To select the Dir List Argument

1. Press **Tab** to select the Tree List window. Select the directory holding the files you want to display by highlighting it with the movement keys.

2. Press **F10**. From the **O**ptions menu, select File **L**ist Filter. Alternatively, press **F8**.

3. Type the file name and the extension to be listed.

   Type **C*** for Name, and **COM** for Ext, for example. This displays all files that begin with C and have the extension .COM.

4. Press **Enter** to display the new list of files.

After you use the Dir List Argument command to select a list of files, you must use the command again to show all files. To display all files in the File List window, select **Reset** in the Dir List Argument dialog box.

To select the Dir List Argument using a mouse

1. Select the directory containing the files to be displayed by clicking it in the Tree List window.

2. From the **Options** menu, click **File List Filter**.

3. Type the file name and the extension to be listed.

4. Click **Select**.

File Map

PCSHELL

Purpose

Displays sectors and clusters used by a file. You select which files you want to see. By viewing the location of your files in this map, you can determine whether your files are fragmented.

Notes

In the File Mapping Service dialog box, each position on the grid represents one cluster. Without exception, DOS allocates one cluster at a time—not sectors—on a disk for a file. However, clusters might be different sizes, depending on the disk you are using.

Each space on the grid, which represents one cluster, displays one of these symbols:

[ ] Available	Cluster is available for file storage.
B Boot record	Cluster contains disk's boot record. Every disk includes a boot record, even if it is not a DOS system disk (one that can start your computer).
F File Alloc Table	Cluster contains File Allocation Table (FAT). DOS uses FAT to keep track of location of files. FAT tells

		DOS where files are stored on disk and which clusters are still available.
D Directory	Cluster is disk's directory.
. Allocated	Cluster is part of a file.
h Hidden	Cluster is part of a hidden file.
r Read Only	Cluster is part of a Read-Only file.
x Bad Cluster	DOS has marked this cluster as bad and has made it unusable.

The File Map command is similar to the Disk Map command. You can locate individual files with the File Map command; you can display on-screen the location of all files on the disk with the Disk Map command.

To use the File Map

1. Select the disk holding the files to be mapped. Press **Ctrl-A**, **Ctrl-B**, or **Ctrl-C** to select drive A, B, or C.

2. Press **Tab** to select the Tree List window. Select the directory containing the file or files you want to map from the Tree List window. Use the movement keys to highlight the directory.

3. Press **Tab** to select the File List window. This window contains the file or files you want to map.

4. Select the file or files you want to map by using the cursor keys to highlight the file name. Press **Enter** to select the file.

   If you do not select any files, PC Shell displays a map for all the files located within the selected subdirectory. You can scroll through the entire list of files by selecting **N**ext within the File Mapping Service dialog box.

5. Press **F10**. From the **S**pecial menu, select **F**ile Map.

6. Select **N**ext to find the next file from the selected subdirectory.

7. Press **Enter** to return to the main PC Shell screen.

To use the File Map using a mouse

1. Select the disk to be mapped by clicking the drive letters in the upper-left corner of the main PC Shell screen.

2. Click anywhere within the File List window to select it.

3. Select the files you want mapped by clicking them.

4. From the **Special** menu, click **File Map**.

5. Click **Next** to display a map of the Next file located within the subdirectory you selected.

6. Click **Exit** to return to the main PC Shell screen.

File Select Filter

PCSHELL

Purpose

The File Select Filter command selects a group of files displayed in the File List window. For example, you can choose to display only files in the subdirectory with the extension .EXE. You can use the standard DOS wild card characters, * and ?, to list files with common file names, extensions, or characters. When you type ***.EXE** in the File Select Filter dialog box, PC Tools displays only those files with the .EXE extension.

Notes

After you use the File Select Filter command to select a list of files, you must use the command again to show all files. To display all files in the File List window, select **Reset** in the File Select Filter dialog box.

To select the File Select Filter

1. Press **Tab** to select the Tree List window. Select the directory holding the files you want to display in

the Tree List window. Use the movement keys to highlight the desired directory.

2. Press **F10**. From the Options Menu, Select File Select Filter.

   Alternatively, Press **F9**.

3. Type the file name and the extension you want to list in the File Select Filter dialog box.

   For example, type **C*** for Name, and **COM** for Ext. This displays all files that begin with C and have the extension .COM.

4. Press **Enter** to display the new list of files.

To use the File Select Filter with a mouse

1. Point to the directory containing the files you want to display.

2. From the **Options** menu, click **File Select Filter**.

3. Type the file name and the extension to be listed.

4. Click **Select**.

═Find

PCSHELL

Purpose

Searches for ASCII or Hex character strings in a file or any number of files. Searches files in the order selected. The maximum size of a search string is 32 characters.

To find a string

1. Select the file or files to be searched. Use the movement keys to highlight the file name. Press **Enter** to select the file.

2. Press **F10**. From the File menu, select Find.

3. Type the search string you want to find in the File Search Service dialog box.

If you are searching for ASCII characters, type the
string of ASCII characters on the ASCII default
line. The ASCII search is not case sensitive. The
matching hexadecimal values appear on the HEX
line.

If you are searching for HEX values, select HEX by
pressing Alt-H. Then type the HEX values on the
Hex default line. The HEX search is case sensitive.
If you type an invalid HEX value, PC Shell beeps.
The matching ASCII values appear on the ASCII
line.

4. Press Alt-B to Begin the search. Any matching
strings located within the file or files appear. If no
matching strings appear on-screen, a message
appears.

5. Select Continue Search to continue the search for
another occurrence after PC Tools finds a string
within a file. Select Edit to edit the sector
containing the matching string. When you finish
searching the file or files, select Cancel to return to
the main PC Shell screen.

To find a character string using a mouse

1. Select the files to be searched by clicking them.

2. From the File menu, click Find.

3. Type the search string you want to find in the File
Search Service dialog box.

If you are searching for ASCII characters, type the
string of ASCII characters on the ASCII default
line. The ASCII search is not case sensitive. The
matching hexadecimal values appear on the HEX
line.

If you are searching for HEX values, click HEX.
Then type the HEX values on the Hex default line.
The HEX search is case sensitive. If you type an
invalid HEX value, PC Shell beeps. The matching
ASCII values appear on the ASCII line.

4. Click Begin to start the search. Any matching
strings located within the file or files appear. If no
matching strings appear on-screen, a message
appears.

5. Click **Continue Search** to continue the search for another occurrence of the string. After you finish searching the file or files, click **Cancel** to return to the main PC Shell screen.

Format Data Disk

PCSHELL

Purpose

Formats disks. Format Data Disk is similar to the DOS FORMAT command. You must format new disks before you use them.

Notes

If you are using PC Shell in the resident mode, you can call PC Shell from within another program to format a disk. Then you can return to your program, without actually exiting your other program.

Format Data Disk initializes each track on the disk so that your computer can recognize it and use it to store your data files. This command destroys any data already stored on your disk.

Use Format Data Disk to format new disks; do not use it to make system-bootable disks (disks that can be used to start your computer). You can create system-bootable disks with the PC Shell by selecting the **Make System Disk** option.

Do not make your disks' system-bootable unless you plan to boot the computer with the disk. Adding the files necessary to make the disk system-bootable uses unnecessary disk space. Choosing the **Bootable** option does not make the disk bootable. This option only reserves space for the system files, which must be loaded separately with the Make System Disk command.

To format a data disk

1. Insert a blank diskette into drive A or B.

2. Press **F10**. From the **D**isk menu, select **F**ormat Data Disk.

3. Select the drive containing the blank disk in the Disk Format dialog box. Press **Enter** to Continue.

4. Select the desired formatting option available within the Disk Initialization Service dialog box. Depending on the computer you are using, one or more of these options may be available:

   • 160K single-sided; 8 sectors per track; 40 tracks

   • 180K single-sided; 9 sectors per track; 40 tracks

   • 320K double-sided; 8 sectors per track; 40 tracks

   • 360K single-sided; 9 sectors per track; 40 tracks

   • 720K 3 1/2-inch diskette; 80 tracks; double sided; 9 sectors per track

   • 1.2M high capacity; 80 tracks; double-sided;15 sectors per track

   • 1.44M high capacity; 80 tracks; double sided;18 sectors per track

   Depending on the computer and version of DOS you are using, you may need to install the DOS DRIVER.SYS in your CONFIG.SYS file before all formatting options are available in the Disk Initialization Service dialog box.

   When a dot appears in the track, that particular track has been successfully formatted. When the disk has been formatted, you return to the main PC Shell menu.

5. Select Format to proceed with the formatting of your disk. The status of the formatting process appears in the Disk Initialization Service dialog box.

6. Type the name of the volume label in the Disk Initialization Service dialog box and select Continue.

7. Select Bootable to make the disk system bootable, or select Skip to return to format another disk or to Exit to the main PC Shell menu.

   If you select Skip, the Disk Initialization Service dialog box displays information about the disk. This information includes the number of bytes of the total disk space, the number of bytes in bad sectors, and the number of bytes available on the disk.

8. Select Next Disk to format another disk or select EXit to return to the main PC Shell menu.

To format a disk using a mouse

1. Insert a blank disk into drive A or B.

2. From the Disk menu, click Format Data Disk.

3. Click the drive containing the disk you want to format.

4. Click one of the available format options displayed within the Disk Initialization Service dialog box.

5. Click Format to start formatting the disk.

6. Type the Volume Label when requested. Click Continue.

7. Click Skip, then select Next Disk or Exit.

Help

DESKTOP, PCSHELL

Purpose

Assists you in locating commands, or offers you a description of what the command does.

Notes

PC Tools Utilities offers Help regardless of where you are in the program. You can access Help at any time by pressing F1.

If a menu is open, information displayed in the Help dialog box describes the commands available. If you select Rename File from a menu, for example, and access Help, the information displayed concerns the Rename File command.

A Help Index is also available when you use PC Shell. This index provides a list of topics where Help is available. You can access the Help Index at any time by pressing **F2**.

To get help

1. Press **F10** and select **Help**. Alternatively, press **F1**.

2. Select **Index** to display a list of other available topics. Move the selection bar to the desired topic menu and press **Enter**.

To get help using a mouse

Click the **Help** menu located at the top of the main PC Shell menu.

Hex Edit

PCSHELL

Purpose

Views inside a file and enables you to edit the contents of the file. Views files in ASCII or HEX values.

Notes

Before you make changes to any file with this command, you should have a working knowledge of ASCII and hexadecimal values, and sector bytes. Making improper changes to your files with the View/Edit command can make your programs inoperable.

To view a file

1. Select the file or files for PC Tools to search. Use the movement keys to highlight the file name. Press **Enter** to select the file.

2. Press **F10**. From the File menu, select **Hex Edit File**.

3. Select **ASCII/HEX** to switch between formatted text mode (ASCII) and HEX mode (primarily used for editing) within the File View/Edit Service dialog box.

4. Select Cancel to return to the main PC Shell screen.

You cannot edit or change a file when it is in formatted text mode.

To edit a file

These key commands are available to assist during the editing process:

Home	Moves to beginning of file
End	Moves to end of file
PgUp	Repositions display several lines backward in file
PgDn	Repositions display several lines forward in file
Esc	Exits to main PC Shell screen

In addition, you use the scroll bars on the right side of the screen with the mouse to scroll through the file.

1. Select the file or files you want to search by using the movement keys to highlight the file name. Press **Enter** to select a file.

2. Press **F10**. From the File menu, select **H**ex Edit File.

3. Select **A**SCII/HEX to switch to HEX mode within the File View Service dialog box.

4. Choose one of these three options:

   • Select **A**SCII/HEX to toggle back to the formatted text (ASCII) display.

   • Select **C**hange Sector to change to a different relative sector within the selected file. Enter the new sector number, then select **C**ontinue to change the sector, or select E**X**it to return to the preceding screen.

   • Select **E**dit to switch to the Sector Edit Service dialog box.

   Select **C**ancel to return to the main PC Shell screen.

To edit a sector

1. Select **E**dit within the File View Service dialog screen.

2. Position the cursor over the first byte you want to edit.

3. Type the new ASCII or Hexadecimal values. The new values replace the original bytes, and appear in color or are highlighted on-screen.

   Press **F8** to make changes by typing in the ASCII column.

4. Select **Save** to write any changes made to the disk.

To repair a bad sector within a file

1. Select **A**SCII/HEX from the File View Service dialog box.

2. Select **E**dit.

3. Select **S**ave to rewrite the same sector information, without the error, onto your disk.

This procedure should make the sector readable, but some information rewritten on the sector may be invalid. This procedure recovers as much of your data as possible.

To view/edit a file using a mouse

1. Click the files you want to view or edit.

2. From the **File** menu, click **View/Edit**.

══ # Keyboard Macros ══════════════

DESKTOP

Purpose

Record a series of keystrokes that you can play back repeatedly by executing a simple command.

Notes

You can use the Macro Editor in other programs, if you have loaded PC Tools Desktop as memory resident. If PC Tools Desktop is not resident in your computer's memory, the macros work only in the Desktop.

As a safety feature, you cannot start some programs by using a macro. For example, a macro cannot start PC Secure, PC Backup, or Compress, which prevents accidental erasure or loss of data to your computer.

To run a macro

To play back a macro, enter a macro key combination (which you assign when you create it). It runs where you positioned the cursor. When the macro stops, you can continue working in the application.

To open the Macro Editor

1. Select **M**acro Editor from the main PC Desktop menu.

2. Select or create a file in the File Load dialog box.

To write a macro

You can write a macro in the Macro Editor window. To do so requires some consideration of what you intend to do with the macro.

In some cases, you must press **F7** before you press the key. If you want to record Backspace as one of the keystrokes in a macro, for example, you must press **F7** and then **Backspace**. F7 means insert the key; by pressing F7, the next key is inserted in the macro, and does not perform the command in the Macro Editor screen.

To begin defining a macro, press **Alt** and the plus (+) key. To end defining a macro, press **Alt** and the minus (-) key. You must contain all macro keystrokes in the < > brackets.

The following is an example of a macro created in the Macro Editor:

<begdef><ctrlq>Memorandum<enddef>

To set macro activation

1. Press **F10**. From the **F**ile menu, select **M**acro Activation. Alternatively, press **F8**.

2. Press **Tab** to select one of the following options:

Not Active	No files play back
Active When in PC Tools Desktop	Macros in current file play back when you are in PC Tools Desktop
Active When Not in PC Tools Desktop	Macros in current file play back except when you are in PC Tools Desktop
Active Everywhere	Macros in current file play back in PC Tools Desktop and in other applications

This option sets whether macros can be used only in PC Desktop, or in other programs.

Locate File

Purpose

Locates a file anywhere on a disk.

Notes

Locate File is especially useful if you remember the name of a file, but cannot remember in which directory the file is located. The Locate File command searches all the directories on the disk, and reports where the file is located.

To locate a file

1. Select the disk you want to search. Press **Ctrl-A**, **Ctrl-B**, or **Ctrl-C** to select drive A, B, or C.

2. Press **F10**. From the **D**isk menu, select **L**ocate File.

3. Type the file name and extension of the file to locate in the File Locator Service dialog box.

4. Press Enter to begin the search process to locate the file.

You can use the wild card characters * and ? to search for similar files or similar names. To search for all files with the extension .WP, for example, type *.WP. The * can represent up to eight characters (either the file name or the extension) and the ? can represent any single character.

The located files display in a wide-screen window. You can use the entire PC Tools menu to work with these files. When you want to return to the normal display, press Esc.

To locate a file using a mouse

1. Select the disk to search by clicking the drive letters in the upper-left corner of the main PC Shell screen.

2. From the Disk menu, click Locate File.

3. Type the name of the file to locate in the File Locator Service dialog box, and click Locate.

Macro Editor Files

DESKTOP

Purpose

Store your macros.

Note

The commands to edit text in the Macro Editor are similar to the commands used in Clipboard and Notepad.

To load macro editor files

1. Press F10. From the File menu, select Load.

2. Select a file from the File Load dialog box.

To save files

1. Press **F10**. From the **F**ile menu, select **S**ave. Alternatively, press **F5**.

2. Press **Alt-S** to save the file.

To use the Autosave feature

1. Press **F10**. From the **F**ile menu, select **A**utosave.

2. Type a number for the amount of minutes you want to lapse between each autosave.

3. Press **Tab** to turn on the automatic save.

4. Press **Alt-O** to set the automatic save.

The Autosave feature automatically saves your files after a specified time.

To search the Macro Editor

1. Press **F10**. From the **S**earch menu, select **F**ind.

2. Type the characters you want to search for in the Find dialog box.

3. You may select from the following options:

Case Sensitive	If turned on, finds exact matches only. If you search for the word *the* and turn on Case Sensitive, for example, Macro Editor ignores the word *THE*.
Whole Words Only	If turned on, Macro Editor searches for words only, not part of a word. If you search for the word *his* and turn on Whole words only, for example, Macro Editor ignores *his* in the word *history*.

4. Press **Alt-F**.

To replace text

1. Press **F10**. From the **S**earch menu, select **R**eplace.

2. Type the characters for which you want to search in the Find dialog box.

3. Type the characters to be replaced in the Find dialog box.

4. You may select one of the following options:

> Replace One Time
> Replace All
> Verify Before Replace
> Case Sensitive
> Whole Words Only

5. Press **Alt-R** to select **R**eplace.

To erase all macros

Press **F10**. From the **C**ontrols menu, select **E**rase all macros.

This command deactivates any current macro.

To set playback delay

1. Press **F10**. From the **C**ontrols menu, select **P**layback delay.

2. Type a number for the amount of time you want the macro delayed.

   Each number represents 1/18th of a second.

3. Press **Tab** to turn on the Macro playback delay.

4. Press **Alt-O** to set the Macro playback delay.

To select the Learn Mode

1. Press **F10**. From the **C**ontrols menu, select **L**earn Mode.

2. Press **Ctrl-Space bar** to exit PC Desktop.

3. Press **Alt-+** to begin recording the macro.

4. Enter the keystroke combination for this macro, such as **Ctrl-G**.

5. Type the commands and keystrokes desired.

6. Press **Alt- -**

You are still in Learn mode until you return to the Macro Editor and turn it off. PC Tools creates a file called LEARN.PRO, which you can edit. You also can paste the macros into separate files that you can run easily.

PC Tools Desktop must be memory resident to use the Learn mode.

To save macro settings

Press F10. From the Controls menu, select Save setup.

To mark a block of text

1. Move the cursor to the location where you want to begin marking text.

2. Press F10. From the Edit menu, select Mark block.

3. Use the movement keys to position the cursor where you want to mark the text in Clipboard.

To unmark a block of text

1. Press Esc. Alternatively, press F10.

2. From the Edit menu, select Unmark block.

To copy to Clipboard

1. Use the movement keys to position the cursor where you want to start copying text into Clipboard.

2. Press F10. From the Edit menu, select Copy.

3. Use the movement keys to mark a block of text to copy into Clipboard.

4. Press Enter to copy the blocked text into Clipboard.

To paste from Clipboard

1. Use the movement keys to position the cursor where you want to paste the text from Clipboard.

2. Press F10. From the Edit menu, select Paste.

To erase a block of text

1. Move the cursor to the location where you want to begin erasing text.

2. Press **F10**. From the **E**dit menu, select **M**ark block.

3. Use the movement keys to position the cursor where you want to mark the text to erase.

4. Press **F10**. From the **E**dit menu, select Cu**T** to clipboard.

To delete all text

1. Press **F10**. From the **E**dit menu, select **D**elete all text.

2. Select **OK** to confirm that all text in Clipboard should be deleted.

To insert a file

1. Use the movement keys to position the cursor where you want to insert a file in Clipboard.

2. Press **F10**. From the **E**dit menu, select **I**nsert file.

3. Select the file to insert from the File Load dialog box.

4. Press **Alt-L** to **L**oad the selected file.

To go to a particular line in the text

1. Press **F10**. From the **E**dit menu, select **G**oto.

2. Type the line number to go to.

3. Press **Enter**.

To find text

The **F**ind and Replace command always searches from the cursor forward in Macro Editor. It does not perform a global search.

1. Move the cursor to the location where you want to begin marking text.

2. Press **F10**. From the **E**dit menu, select **M**ark block.

3. Use the movement keys to position the cursor where you want to mark the text in Clipboard.

Make System Disk

PCSHELL

Purpose

Transfers the DOS system files to a formatted disk. After PC Tools places the system files on the formatted disk, you can use that disk to start your computer.

The disk you use to make a system disk must be blank, because one of the system files must be positioned in an exact location on the disk. If any other file is using that location on the disk, this command does not work. If a problem occurs in making a system disk, PC Shell reports the error to you during the command.

To make a system disk

1. Insert a blank, formatted disk into drive A or B.

2. Press **F10**. From the **D**isk menu, select Make S**Y**stem Disk.

3. Select drive **A** or **B** from the Make System Disk dialog box.

4. Press **Enter** to **C**ontinue after selecting the drive.

5. Press **Enter** to confirm that you want to make a system disk in the Make a System Diskette Service dialog box.

To make a system disk using a mouse

1. Insert a blank, formatted disk into drive A or drive B.

2. From the **D**isk menu, click **Make System Disk**

3. Select drive **A** or **B** from the Make System Disk dialog box by clicking your choice.

4. Click **Continue**.

5. Click **Continue** to confirm that you want to make a system disk in the Make a System Diskette Service dialog box.

Memory Map

Purpose

Displays type, location, and size of DOS memory blocks and the names of the applications using those blocks. Memory Map is useful when you need to know which programs are loaded into your computer's memory and how much memory each program is using.

Memory Map offers four choices on how to display the memory map:

Item	Description
Show only program memory blocks	Maps only the blocks occupied by programs
Show only program memory blocks with "hooked" vectors	Maps just the blocks occupied by programs, and displays any system vectors pointing to that block
Show all memory blocks	Maps all memory blocks
Show all memory blocks with "hooked" vectors	Maps all memory blocks and displays any system vectors pointing to that block

You can select any one of these options when using the Memory Map. When the Memory Map is displayed, this information appears on-screen:

Enter	Type of memory control blocks
Prog	Application Program
Sys	System program
Env	DOS environment
Free	Unallocated memory
Paragraphs	Memory area used by program

Bytes	Number of bytes in computer's memory used by program
Owner	Name of the program in your computer's memory

To run Memory Map

1. Press F10. From the Special menu, select MEmory Map.

2. Select your preference of Mapping technique within the Memory Mapping Service dialog box by pressing 1, 2, 3, or 4.

3. Select Map.

4. Press Enter to select Map, which returns you to the Memory Map Service dialog box.

   Alternatively, select EXit to return to the main PC Shell screen.

To run Memory Map using a mouse

1. From the Special menu, click Memory Map.

2. Click your preference of Mapping technique; then click Map.

3. Click Map or Exit.

Message Bar

PCSHELL

Purpose

Provides additional information, keystroke options, or help. The Message Bar is located at the very bottom of the PC Shell screen. The Message bar constantly changes, depending on where you are working in PC Shell. You execute the commands that appear on the message linewith the function keys.

To use the Message Bar

Press any function key displayed on the Message Bar to execute the associated commands.

For example, from the main PC Shell screen, the following commands are available from the Message Bar:

F1	Help
F2	Index
F3	Exit
F4	Unselect
F5	Info
F6	Display
F7	Switch
F8	List
F9	Select
F10	Menu

 **Mirror**

MIRROR

Purpose

Keeps a backup copy of the File Allocation Table (FAT) and the root directory of your hard disk in a special hidden file.

Notes

Use only if you accidentally damage files on your disk by running DOS ERASE, RECOVER, or FORMAT.

Use MIRROR with REBUILD to recover the disk if a major disaster of lost data occurs from the accidental use of the DOS commands.

Run MIRROR often. You may want to consider placing MIRROR in AUTOEXEC.BAT. REBUILD can recover only those files reported in Mirror. To ensure that all files can be recovered by REBUILD if the need ever arises, run MIRROR on a regular basis.

Refer to REBUILD for more information.

To run Mirror

Type **MIRROR** at the DOS prompt.

Modify Applications List

Purpose

Changes the list of programs displayed in the
Applications pull-down menu. You can add, delete, or
edit the applications displayed in the menu. You can
start WordPerfect from the Applications menu, for
example, if you use the Modify Applications List
command first.

Notes

Within the Modify Applications List Service dialog box,
there are seven possible commands. Choose one of these
commands:

Next	Displays next application on list
Prev	Displays previous application on list
Edit	Edits current application's information
NeW	Adds application programs to Applications menu
Del	Deletes application programs from Applications menu
Save	Saves Applications list
EXit	Ends Modify Applications List command and returns to main PC Shell screen

---
To add or edit an application

If you choose to add or edit an application so that you
can run a program from the Applications menu within

PC Shell, the following options are available within the
Modify Applications List Service.

Use the caret symbol (^) by pressing **Shift-6** before a
letter to highlight that letter. You then can use the
highlighted letter to start the application from the
keyboard.

Title
: Area where you type text you want
to appear on the Applications menu
to represent the program.

Initial
Directory
: Specifies path where application
and its associated files are located
on the drive. Resets current
directory when program is run so it
can find its files. If the subdirectory
is included in the DOS path, this
option is not necessary.

Execute
Path
: Specifies path where application
executes.

Run
File Name
: Lists exact name and extension
used to start application program.

Run
Parameter(s)
: Adds any start-up switches you
want to pass on to a program.

Wait
on Last
Screen?
: Pauses screen before returning
to the main PC Shell menu. This is
helpful because you can see the
screen when you run a program that
does not pause the screen before it
ends (for example, CHKDSK).
Respond Yes or No to this
question.

Run with
selected
menu
file?
: Runs program using selected
file. If EDLIN is in Applications
pull-down menu and you select
a text file in the File List window,
for example, the selected text file
passes through to the editor when
it is run. You can then begin to
edit the file. Respond Yes or No
to this question.

| Pull down Application Menu initially? | If set to Yes, displays Application menu on start-up, and the menu remains pulled down. This option sets the same for all files in your Application list. Enter Yes or No for this option. |
| File extension associations | Specifies any file extensions that automatically start the associated program. If you enter dBASE IV into your Application menu with a file extension association of .dbf, for example, you can run your dBASE IV program, and dBASE IV automatically starts with the selected database file loaded. |

To modify the applications list

1. Press **F10**. From the Options menu, select Modify Applications List.

2. Select Next, Prev, Edit, NeW, Del, or Save.

3. If you choose New or Edit, type the information about your application program in the Modify Applications List Service dialog box.

4. Select Save.

5. Select EXit to return to the main PC Shell menu.

To modify applications list using a mouse

1. From the **Options** menu, select **Modify Applications List**.

2. Click **Next, Prev, Edit, New, Del, Save,** or **Edit**.

3. If you choose **New** or **Edit**, type the information about your application program in the Modify Applications List Service dialog box.

4. Click **Save**.

5. Click **Exit** to return to the main PC Shell menu.

More File Info

PCSHELL

Purpose

Provides more specific information about a file. Lists the file name, its extension, the file path, any attributes assigned to the file, the last time the file was accessed, the file length, the total number of clusters the file occupies, and the cluster number. You can select more than one file.

To see more file information

1. Press **Tab** to select the Tree List window. Select the directory containing the file or files on which you want more information in the Tree List window. Use the movement keys to highlight the directory.

2. Press **Tab** to select the File List window. This window contains the file or files on which you want more information.

3. Select the file or files on which you want more information by using the movement keys to highlight the file name. Press **Enter** to select the file.

4. Press **F10**. From the File menu, select More File Info.

5. Select **EX**it to return to the main PC Shell screen. Select **N**ext to display more file information on the next file, if you selected more than one file.

To see more file information using a mouse

1. Select the files to view or edit by clicking them.

2. From the **File** menu, click **More File Info**.

3. Click **Exit** to return to the main PC Shell screen.

Move File

Purpose

Moves one or many files.

Notes

You can move the files to the same drive but into another directory, to the same drive but with a different or new file name, or from one drive to another. Move functions similar to Copy, except that it automatically deletes the moved file or files from the original drive or directory after a successful copy.

To move files

1. Press **Tab** to select the Tree List window. Select the directory containing the file or files from which you want to move. Use the movement keys to highlight the directory.

2. Press **Tab** to select the File List window. This window contains the file or files you want to move.

3. Select the file or files you want to move by using the movement keys to highlight the file name. Press **Enter** to select the file.

4. Press **F10**. From the File menu, select Move.

5. To confirm the Move command press **Enter** to Continue. This message box warns you that the Move command will delete the source file or files.

   If you are using the single-list display, go to Step 6.

   If you are using the two-list display to move, PC Shell displays a message asking whether the second or other window is the one where you want the files to be moved. If it is, Press **Enter** to select Yes. A dialog box appears, and PC Tools moves the files.

   If you do not want to move the files to the second window, select No. Continue with Step 6.

6. Select the target drive in the File Move box by pressing the **down arrow**. Press **Enter** to Continue.

If the target drive contains subdirectories

Press **Tab** to select the Tree List Window. Select the directory where you want to move the file or files in the Tree List window.

If the target drive contains files with the same file names that you are moving, perform one of the following steps:

- Select **Replace All** to replace all files in the target directory with the same names as the moved files.

- Select **Replace File** to replace the current file in the target with the same name as the moved file.

- Select **Next File** to skip to the next file you want to move. Current file does not move.

- Select **Skip All** to skip all the files you want to move, and to return to the main PC Shell screen.

Select EXit to return to the main PC Shell screen.

If the selected target drive is the same as the source drive, the File Move Service dialog box appears with the message `Cannot move file to same path`. Press **Enter** to select EXit.

The files move to the new location (the target). PC Tools then returns to the main PC Shell screen.

To move files using a mouse

1. Click anywhere within the Tree List window to select it.

2. Click the directory containing the file or files you want to move.

3. Click anywhere within the File List window to select it.

4. Select the files you want moved (the source) by clicking them.

5. Position the mouse cursor onto one of the selected files. Press **Ctrl**, then click the **left button** on the mouse.

6. Drag the file name to the target directory in the Tree List window. A Move box appears and moves

with the mouse cursor. The Move box displays the number of files PC Tools is moving.

7. Release the mouse button. A message box appears asking you to confirm the Move command. Click **Continue** to start the moving process.

Notepads

DESKTOP

Purpose

Performs simple word processing.

Notes

Since PC Tools Desktop can be memory resident, there is instant access to the word processor. A notepad file, compatible with WordStar files, can hold approximately 60,000 characters.

These keyboard commands are available when working in Notepad:

Key	Effect
(Any character)	Inserts character at cursor
Backspace	Erases character left of cursor
Delete	Deletes character at cursor
Enter	Inserts paragraph at cursor
Space bar	Inserts space at cursor
Tab	Inserts tab at cursor
Up arrow	Moves cursor up one line
Down arrow	Moves cursor down one line
Left arrow	Moves cursor left one character
Right arrow	Moves cursor right one character

Ctrl- left arrow or **Home**	Moves to beginning of line
Ctrl- right arrow or **End**	Moves to end of line
Ctrl-Home	Moves to beginning of file
Ctrl-End	Moves to end of file
Home (pressed twice)	Moves to beginning of window
End (pressed twice)	Moves to end of window
PgUp	Scrolls text up one window
PgDn	Scrolls text down one window
Ctrl-PgUp	Scrolls up one line without moving cursor
Ctrl-PgDn	Scrolls down one line without moving cursor

To load a Notepad file

1. Press **F10**. From the **F**ile menu, select **L**oad.

2. Select the file in the Load Form dialog box.

3. Press **Alt-L** to load the form.

To save a Notepad file

1. Press **F10**. From the **F**ile menu, select **S**ave.

2. Press **Tab** to select any of the following options:

   • **PC Tools Desktop** saves file in PC Tools Desktop file format

   • **ASCII** saves file as regular ASCII file

   • **Make Backup File** creates second file or backup file with same file name, but uses the extension .BAK.

3. Press **Alt-S** to select **S**ave.

To print a Notepad file

1. Press **F10**. From the **F**ile menu, select **P**rint.

2. Press **Tab** to select any of the following options:

   - **Device**—LPT1, LPT2, or LPT3; COM1, COM2, Disk File

   - **Number**—Type a number the number of copies you want

3. To start the printing, press **Enter** to select **P**rint.

To use the Autosave feature

1. Press **F10**. From the **F**ile menu, select **A**utosave.

2. Type a number for the amount of minutes you want to lapse between each autosave.

3. Press **Tab** to turn on the automatic save.

4. Press **Alt-O** to set the automatic save.

Autosave automatically saves your files after a specified time.

To exit without saving

Press **F10**. From the **F**ile menu, select E**X**it PC Shell.

This option does not save your changes made in the Notepad window.

To edit Notepad text

Use the basic edit keyboard commands, or use the mouse to position the cursor.

To cut text to Clipboard

1. Move the cursor to the location you want to begin cutting text.

2. Press **F10**. From the **E**dit menu, select **M**ark Block.

3. Use the movement keys to move the cursor to where you want to mark the text you want to erase.

4. Press **F10**. From the **E**dit menu, select Cu**T** to Clipboard.

   Alternatively, press **Shift-Del**.

To copy text to Clipboard

1. Use the movement keys to position the cursor where you want to start copying text into Clipboard.

2. Press **F10**. From the **E**dit menu, select **M**ark Block.

   The cursor changes shape to a large block cursor.

3. Use the movement keys to mark a block of text to copy to Clipboard.

4. Press **F10**. From the **E**dit menu, select **C**opy to Clipboard.

To paste text from the Clipboard

1. Use the movement keys to position the cursor where you want to paste the text from Clipboard.

2. Press **F10**. From the **E**dit menu, select **P**aste from Clipboard.

Text placed in Clipboard remains there until it is replaced or until the program ends.

To mark a block of text

1. Move the cursor to the location where you want to begin marking text.

2. Press **F10**. From the **E**dit menu, select **M**ark Block.

3. Use the movement keys to position the cursor where you want to mark the text in Clipboard.

To unmark a block of text

Press **Esc**. Alternatively, press **F10**. From the **E**dit menu, select **U**nmark Block.

To delete all text

1. Press **F10**. From the **E**dit menu, select **D**elete All Text.

2. Select **OK** to confirm that you want all text in Clipboard deleted.

To insert a file

1. Use the movement keys to move the cursor to where you want to insert a file in Clipboard.

2. Press **F10**. From the **E**dit menu, select **I**nsert File.

3. Select the file to insert from the File Load dialog box.

4. Press **Alt-L** to load the selected file.

To use the Goto command

1. Press **F10**. From the **E**dit menu, select **G**oto.

2. Type the line number of your destination.

3. Press **Enter**.

The Goto command enables you to move to a specified line in the Notepad.

To check the spelling of a word

1. Use the movement keys to move the cursor to the word you want to spell check.

2. Press **F10**. From the **E**dit menu, select Spellcheck **W**ord.

3. Select one of the following options if Spellcheck finds any misspelled words:

Ignore	Disregards word
Correct	Displays Word Correction dialog box, which enables you to select correct word from a list of possible words
Add	Adds word to dictionary
Quit	Exits spell check option

To check the spelling of a screen

1. Use the movement keys to move the cursor to the screen you want to spell check.

2. Press **F10**. From the **E**dit menu, select Spellcheck Screen.

3. Select **I**gnore, **C**orrect, **A**dd, or **E**xit if any misspelled words are detected.

To check the spelling of a file

1. Press **F10**. From the **E**dit menu, select Spellcheck **F**ile.

2. Select **I**gnore, **C**orrect, **A**dd, or **E**xit if Spellcheck finds any misspelled words in the file.

Note

The Find and Replace command always searches from the cursor forward in Notepad. It does not perform a global search.

To find text

1. Press **F10**. From the **S**earch menu, select **F**ind.

2. Type the characters for which you want to search in the Find dialog box.

3. Select one the following options:

Case Sensitive	If turned on, finds exact matches only. If you search for *the* and turn on Case Sensitive, for example, Notepad ignores the word *THE*.
Whole Words Only	If turned on, Notepad searches for words only, not part of a word. If you search for *his* and turn on Whole Words Only, for example, Notepad ignores *his* in the word *history*.

4. Press **Alt-F**.

To replace text

1. Press **F10**. From the **S**earch menu, select **R**eplace.

2. Type the characters for which you want to search in the Find dialog box.

3. Type the characters to replace in the Find dialog box.

4. You may select one of the following options:

   Replace One Time
   Replace All
   Verify Before Replace
   Case Sensitive
   Whole Words Only

5. Press **Alt-R**.

To set the page layout

1. Press **F10**. From the Controls menu, select Page Layout.

2. Set the margins, paper size, line spacing, and starting page number.

3. Select OK by pressing **Alt-O**.

To create a header/footer

1. Press **F10**. From the Controls menu, select Header/Footer.

2. Type the header and footer in the Page Header & Footer dialog box.

3. Select OK by pressing **Alt-O**.

To save your Notepad setup

Press **F10**. From the Controls menu, select Save Setup.

To edit the tab ruler

1. Press **F10**. From the Controls menu, select Tab Ruler Edit.

2. Press the **left-** or **right-arrow** key to move the cursor position on the tab ruler.

3. Press **Ins** to set a tab.

4. Press **Esc** to continue working.

To set even-spaced tabs

1. Press F10. From the Controls menu, select Tab Ruler Edit.

2. Type a number between 3 and 29.

3. Press Esc to continue working.

To delete a tab

1. Press F10. From the Controls menu, select Tab Ruler Edit.

2. Press the left- or right-arrow key to move the cursor position on the tab ruler.

3. Press Del to delete a tab.

4. Press Esc to continue working.

To switch to Overtype mode

Press F10. From the Controls menu, select Overtype mode.

Overtype mode is similar to Replace mode. Anything you type replaces or types over previously entered text.

To display control characters

Press F10. From the Controls menu, select Control Char display.

The Control Char display shows the carriage returns, tabs, and space characters in the text.

To use Wordwrap

Press F10. From the Controls menu, select Wordwrap.

Turn on Wordwrap so that text on each line automatically wraps to the next line. When Wordwrap is on, you do not have to press Enter at the end of each line.

To turn on Auto Indent

Press F10. From the Controls menu, select Auto Indent.

When Auto Indent is turned on, the text automatically indents according to the tab setting, and the entire paragraph aligns on that tab setting.

One List Display

Purpose

Closes the second set of Tree and File List windows. Closes the inactive set of windows, and returns you to a one list display.

Notes

The second set of Tree and File List windows was created under the Two List Display command, located within the Options menu.

Use the Save Configuration command located in the Options menu to save the One List Display settings for your next PC Shell sessions.

To switch to a one list display

Press F10. From the Options menu, select One List Display.

Alternatively, press Del.

To switch to a one list display using a mouse

From the Options menu, click One List Display.

Outlines

Purpose

Helps organize ideas. Automatically assigns a level to each line of text.

Notes

You can use this option from the Desktop to prepare notes for a meeting, or to prepare a presentation or speech. An outline consists of different lines of text, each representing a main idea, followed by other more specific, abbreviated information.

Use **Tab** and **Backspace** to establish and change the different levels in Outline. You can add new levels of the outline easily by moving the cursor, pressing **Enter**, and tabbing to set the new level.

To create an outline

1. Select Outlines from the main Desktop menu.

2. Type the name of the outline in the File Load dialog box.

   The outline file name must contain the .OUT extension.

3. Select New to start the outline.

Park Disk

PCSHELL

Purpose

Parks the read/write head of a hard disk drive over an unused portion of the hard disk. Prevents loss of data or damage to your hard disk that can occur if the head bounces on the surface of the hard disk.

Be sure to use this command before you move your computer.

To park a hard disk drive

1. Press **F10**. From the Disk menu, select Park Disk.

2. Turn off the power to your computer.

The hard disk head is parked at the highest unused cylinder on the drive.

To park a hard disk drive using a mouse

1. From the Disk menu, click Park Disk.

2. Turn off the power to your computer.

=|PC Backup|

PCBACKUP

Purpose

Makes a backup copy of your hard disk. Separate utility program with PC Tools Deluxe.

Notes

PC Backup is a separate utility program included with PC Tools Deluxe. This program features high speed, data compression, support of all sizes of disks, error recovery, verification after writing, disk/time estimates, directory tree display, include and exclude parameters, named backups, and on-line help.

High Speed Direct Memory Access (DMA) makes your backup run faster, but this works only when backing up to floppy disks. If you use DMA, you cannot use the standard DOS DIR command. To see the directory listing of files on a disk where you used DMA, you can use the utility PCBDIR.COM file.

To use PC Backup

Type PCBACKUP at the DOS prompt, and press Enter.

To back up your hard drive

1. Press F10. From the Configure menu, select Define Drive Types.

2. Press Tab to select the type of drive you are using to copy the backup file information.

3. Select OK.

4. Press F10. From the Backup menu, select Backup From Entry.

5. Type C:\ and press Enter to back up drive C.

6. Press Enter to Exit the Backup directory entry.

7. Press F10. From the Backup menu, select Backup Type.

8. Press Tab to select Full Mode and High Speed DMA Method.

9. Press Alt-O to continue.

10. Press F10. From the Backup menu, select Backup To entry.

11. Press Tab to select the drive to which you want to back up.

12. Press Alt-O to continue.

13. Press F10. From the Backup menu, select Start Backup.

14. Insert disks into your drive as prompted.

    Always label each disk (#1, #2, #3, and so on) when making a backup of your hard drive.

15. Press Enter to select OK when the backup is complete.

16. Press F10. From the Configure menu, select Save as Default to save these settings.

_____

To restore data to your hard drive

1. Press F10. From the Restore menu, select Start Restore.

2. Insert your backup disks into your drive as prompted.

    During the Restore, PC Backup may find the original file on your hard drive. If this happens and if you have selected Overwrite Warning in the Options menu, PC Backup displays a Warning! dialog box. Select Overwrite by pressing Alt-O to continue.

3. Select OK to continue.

You can save the setup and load a setup using PC Backup. This is useful to assign a name to a backup session. If you are backing up your hard drive daily, for example, you could assign MONDAY, TUESDAY, WEDNESDAY, THURSDAY, and FRIDAY as names. Then, each day, select that day's name as a setup. As a timesaver, simply type **PCBACKUP MONDAY** to run Monday's regular backup.

To save a PC BACKUP setup

1. Press **F10**. From the Options menu, select Save Setup.

2. Type the name of the setup, and select OK.

To load a setup

1. Press **F10**. From the Options menu, select Load setup.

2. Press **Tab** to select the setup to use.

3. Press **Alt-O** to select OK.

PC-Cache

PC-CACHE

Purpose

Speeds up your programs. By speeding up hard and floppy disk access, PC-Cache reduces the number of times your computer has to wait for the disk when reading data. PC-Cache also writes to the disk, avoiding loss of information.

To run PC-Cache

To run PC-Cache, type

   PC-CACHE

at the DOS prompt, and press **Enter**.

When running PC-Cache, the following optional parameters also are available.

/ID

Specifies a drive to ignore caching, where *d* is the drive letter. PC-Cache caches all drives it can find.

For example, type

PC-CACHE /IB

to run PC-Cache, except on drive B.

/SIZE=*nnn*K

Specifies the amount of standard memory (in 1k increments) to allocate to PC-Cache. If no size is given, PC-Cache defaults to 64K. The maximum size is 512K.

/SIZEXP=*nnn*K

Specifies the amount of expanded memory to allocate to PC-Cache.

/SIZEXT=*nnn*K

Specifies the amount of extended memory to allocate to PC-Cache. This option is only available with computers using 286 and 386 processors.

You can use only one size option. Sizes cannot be mixed among standard, expanded, and extended memory. The minimum size that you can specify is 64K.

/EXTSTART=*nnnn*K

Specifies the start location of the cache buffer in extended memory. EXTSTART must be greater than 1M (1024K). This option is only required if other programs besides VDISK are using extended memory.

/FLUSH

Flushes the cache and sets it to empty.

/MAX

Specifies the number of sectors that the cache can save from a single read request. When a large program or data file is initially read into the computer's memory, it might consume all the cache buffers. Selecting a lower number (for example, 8-16) optimizes the caching for larger applications.

/MEASURES

Causes a display of the following measurements of PC-Cache's performance:

Logical transfers	The number of data transfers that have occurred between the cache and the current application.
Physical transfers	The number of data transfers that have occurred between the disk and the current application.
Transfers saved	The number of physical transfers saved by PC-Cache. (This is the difference between the logical and the physical transfers.)
Percentage saved	The percentage of transfers saved by PC-Cache.

/NOBATCH

Use only when caching in extended memory. PC-Cache normally transfers four sectors of data at a time. The /NOBATCH parameter reduces that number to one.

This option is recommended when running communications software.

/PARAM

Displays the parameters currently in effect.

/PARAM*

Displays information such as whether EMS memory is available on the computer, the drives available and their sizes, how extended memory is allocated, and so on.

/UNLOAD

Unloads the cache.

Examples

The following examples demonstrate how to enter the command at the DOS prompt:

PC-CACHE/IA/SIZE=128K

creates a cache of 124K that ignores drive A in standard memory.

PC-CACHE/SIZEXP=64K

creates a cache of 64K in expanded memory.

PC Format

PCFORMAT

Purpose

Replaces the DOS FORMAT.COM program. There are several differences between DOS FORMAT.COM and PCFORMAT.COM. DOS Format overwrites anything on a floppy disk, but PC Format first attempts to read the disk. If data is on the floppy disk, PC Format does not overwrite it. On a hard disk, DOS does not actually overwrite the data (unless you are using COMPAQ DOS, AT&T DOS, and some versions of Burroughs DOS). PC Format saves the file name in the directory, changing the first character in the file name.

To run PC Format

At the DOS prompt, type

PCFORMAT A:

You can add regular DOS switches to the command line. For example,

PCFORMAT A: /S

formats the disk and copies the system onto the disk.

Warning

Do not type **PCFORMAT C:**, because this command will format your hard disk, erasing all data stored on it.

PC Secure

PCSECURE

Purpose

Adds a high level of security to sensitive or confidential files stored on your computer's disks. Encrypts, compresses, and hides files on your disk.

Caution

This program can be the equivalent of a paper shredder. If you operate it improperly, you can lose your data forever. You must remember your password, or you may never be able to retrieve the data again.

To run PC Secure

Type

PCSECURE

at the DOS prompt, and press **Enter**.

To encrypt (scramble) a file

1. Press **F10**. From the **F**ile menu, select **E**ncrypt.

2. Select the file to encrypt in the File Selection dialog box.

3. Type your password in the Key Input dialog box.

4. Type your password again to confirm it.

To decrypt (unscramble) a file

1. Press **F10**. From the **F**ile menu, select **D**ecrypt.

2. Select the file to decrypt in the File Selection dialog box.

3. Press **Alt-D** to Decrypt.

4. Type your password in the dialog box.

5. Re-type your password to verify it.

PC Setup

PCSETUP

Purpose

Automatically loads PC Tools Deluxe onto your hard disk.

To run PC Setup

1. Insert PC Tools Deluxe disk number 1 in drive A. Alternatively, you can place disk number 1 in drive B.

2. Type **A:** and press **Enter.**

3. Type **PCSETUP** and press **Enter.**

4. Follow the instructions on your computer screen.

PC Shell

PCSHELL

Purpose

Performs routine and advanced DOS maintenance commands. Operating in a window environment, PC Shell copies, moves, deletes, and compares files, directories, and disks. Also edits, maps, and recovers files.

Notes

Keyboard commands as well as mouse support are available when working in PC Shell.

Press **Tab** to select options or buttons in a dialog box. If a letter is highlighted, press **Alt** and the highlighted

letter to execute the option or command. If a box is
highlighted, you can also press **Enter** to select it.

When working in PC Shell, press **Esc** or **F3** to cancel a
message or dialog box.

To start PC Shell

At the DOS prompt, type

> **PCSHELL**

and press **Enter**.

To load PC Shell as a memory resident program

If your computer has enough memory, you can load PC
Shell into your computer's memory. This is referred to
as running PC Shell as memory resident or in TSR
mode. To load PC Shell as memory resident, start PC
Shell at the DOS prompt by typing

> **PCSHELL /R**

If you are using PC Shell as memory resident, you can
use the hotkey **Ctrl-Esc** to activate PC Shell.

Print

PCSHELL

Purpose

Prints the contents of one or more files.

Print options

There are three print options available with the **P**rint
command:

Print as a standard text file	Prints standard ASCII character text file
Print file using PC Shell print options	Defines the page layout for printing and prints standard text file

Dump each sector in ASCII and HEX	Prints sectors in hexadecimal and ASCII format

To enhance the appearance of a printed page

Choose from the following options in the File Print Service dialog box:

Lines per page	Defines actual number of lines on page.
Margin lines top	Defines number of lines for top and bottom margins.
Extra spaces between lines	Specifies number of blank lines between each printed line.
Left Margin	Determines first print position of line.
Right Margin	Specifies last print position of line.
Page headings	Prints header on each page. Prompts you to enter header text.
Page footings	Prints footer on each page. Prompts you to enter footer text.
Page numbers	Numbers each page.
Stop between pages	Stops printing after each page. Used to print single sheets.
Eject last page	Ejects last page printed.

To print a file

1. Select the files you want to print.

2. Press **F10**. From the **F**ile menu, select **P**rint.

3. Select one of the three print options displayed in the File Print Service dialog box.

4. Press **Enter** to select **P**rint.

5. Select any desired options displayed in the File Print Service dialog box.

6. Press Enter to Continue and to start printing the selected files.

Print Directory

Purpose

Prints complete file list for any selected subdirectory. The list contains file names, size, number of disk clusters, date, time, and any attributes assigned to the files.

To print a directory listing

1. Press Tab to select the Tree List window. Select the directory containing the files you want to list in the Tree List window. Use the movement keys to highlight the directory.

2. Press F10. From the File menu, select PrinT Directory.

Quick Run

Purpose

Sets how much memory PC Shell uses when running, and determines whether to permit you to swap your computer's memory with other programs.

Notes

When you use the Quick Run command, PC Shell does not free up any of your computer's memory prior to running an application. By not swapping memory, your programs should run faster.

PC Shell uses approximately 170K of memory. If your programs require more memory than your computer has available, you may need to set Quick Run off.

The Quick Run command is available only if you are running PC Shell from the DOS command line; it is not available if you are running PC Shell in TSR mode, and you have used the hotkey (Ctrl-Esc) to enter the main PC Shell screen.

You toggle Quick Run on or off. A check mark appears if Quick Run is set on, and no check mark is visible if Quick Run is set off.

To use Quick Run

Press F10. From the O ptions menu, select Q uick Run.

To operate Quick Run using a mouse

From the Options menu, click Quick Run.

Rebuild

REBUILD

Purpose

Recovers files on your hard disk that you have accidentally deleted by using the DOS DEL, ERASE, RECOVER, or FORMAT command.

Rebuilds your File Allocation Table and root directory from information in the MIRROR file.

Cautions

Use only when a disaster occurs and you have accidentally deleted files on your hard disk by using the DOS ERASE, RECOVER, or FORMAT command.

Do not experiment with the Rebuild command. This program rebuilds your File Allocation Tale and root directory from information in the mirror file. You could lose the use of your files if you unnecessarily run Rebuild. Hopefully, you will never need to run Rebuild.

Note

If you are using an AT&T, Burroughs, or Compaq
computer, Rebuild cannot recover lost data that you
accidentally deleted by using the FORMAT.COM file.
On these computers, FORMAT.COM erases the disk, so
that there is nothing left to recover. It is a good idea to
delete FORMAT.COM from your hard disk, and use the
PCFORMAT.COM that is included with PC Tools.

To run Rebuild

Type

   REBUILD C:

and press **Enter**.

(This assumes that you need to rebuild drive C. You can
insert another drive letter if necessary.)

Remove PC Shell

PCSHELL

Purpose

Removes the PC Shell program from your computer's
memory when it is running in TSR mode.

Notes

You must load PC Shell into your computer's memory
before you can use Remove PC Shell. In addition, you
must switch into PC Shell from the DOS prompt by
using a hotkey before you can use this command.

The Remove PC Shell command also removes PC Tools
Desktop from your computer's memory if it was the last
TSR program you loaded.

Caution

If you loaded other TSR programs after loading PC
Shell into your computer's memory, unpredictable
results can occur when you use Remove PC Shell. Be

sure to remove the other TSR program before using this command.

To remove PC Shell

1. At the DOS prompt, press **Ctrl-Esc**.

2. Press **F10**. From the Special menu, select Remove PC Shell.

3. Select Remove.

You can remove PC Shell from your computer's memory by typing

   KILL

at any DOS prompt.

To remove PC Shell using a mouse

1. At the DOS prompt, press **Ctrl-Esc**.

2. From the Special menu, click **Remove PC Shell**.

3. Click **Remove**.

Rename File

PCSHELL

Purpose

Renames a file or many files. Similar to the DOS REN command.

To rename a file

1. Select the file you want to move by using the movement keys to highlight the file name. Press **Enter** to select the file.

2. Press **F10**. From the File menu, select Rename.

3. The current file name and extension is displayed within the File Rename Service dialog box. Choose one of the following three options:

- Select Rename to rename the file. Type the new file name and extension within the File Rename Service dialog box.

- Select Next File to skip the current selected file and display the next file.

- Select Cancel to end the Rename command, and return to the main PC Shell screen.

To rename a file using a mouse

1. Select the file you want to rename by clicking it.

2. From the File menu, click Rename.

3. Follow the preceding instructions to rename additional files.

Rename Volume

PCSHELL

Purpose

Renames the disk volume label. Similar to the DOS LABEL command.

To rename a volume

1. Select the disk to be renamed. Press Ctrl-A, Ctrl-B, or Ctrl-C to select drive A, B, or C.

2. Press F10. From the Disk menu, select Rename Volume.

3. Type the new name of the disk in the Disk Rename Service dialog box. The volume name may contain up to 11 characters.

4. Press Alt-R (Rename) to accept the new volume name.

To rename a volume using a mouse

1. Select the volume by clicking the drive letters in the upper-left corner of the main PC Shell screen.

2. From the **Disk** menu, click **Rename Volume**.

3. Type the new name of the disk in the Disk Rename
   Service dialog box, and click **Rename**.

Re-Read the Tree

PCSHELL

Purpose

Forces PC Shell to re-read the DOS tree, and to revise
the display of the DOS tree.

To re-read the tree

Press **F10**. From the **O**ptions menu, select Re-rea**D** the
Tree.

Reset Selected File

PCSHELL

Purpose

Unselects all selected files in active File List window.

To reset selected files

Press **F10**. From the **O**ptions menu, select **R**eset
Selected Files.

Alternatively, Press **F4**.

To reset selected files using a mouse

From the **Options** menu, click **Reset Selected Files**.

Running Programs

Purpose

Runs other programs from the PC Shell main screen.

Notes

You can run other programs from the PC Shell main
screen if you are running PC Shell in TSR mode from
another program, and you called up PC Shell from the
DOS prompt. You cannot use the hotkey Ctrl-Esc to
enter PC Shell except at the DOS prompt, nor can you
enter PC Shell from the PC Tools Desktop menu. Your
other progams cannot run if you are running PC Shell in
TSR mode.

When you finish running the other program, you are
returned to the PC Shell main screen. Depending on the
program you are running, you might be prompted to
press another key or a mouse button to return to PC
Shell.

To use Running Programs

To run another program, simply select it from the
Applications menu.

For more information about adding applications to the
Applications menu, see Modify Applications List.

Save Configuration

Purpose

Saves all PC Shell options you select. Saves you from
reentering the commands each time you use PC Shell. If
you change screen colors, for example, you can display
the new colors each time you use PC Shell.

To save a new configuration

Press **F10**. From the **O**ptions menu, select **S**ave Configuration.

To save a new configuration using a mouse

From the Options menu, click Save Configuration.

To reset configuration settings

To reset the configuration to its original settings after it has been saved, delete the file PCSHELL.CFG.

Screen Colors

PCSHELL

Purpose

Changes the colors you see on your computer screen. Enables you to set or change the colors according to your preference.

Notes

Your computer hardware determines the colors you see on your computer screen. This command does not work if you are using a monochrome computer display.

To set screen colors

1. Press **F10**. From the **O**ptions menu, select Screen Colors.

2. Use the down arrow to select the item with the color you want to change.

3. Type the number (0-7) of the new color.

4. Press Alt-O to accept the new screen colors.

To set screen colors using a mouse

1. From the Options menu, click Screen Colors.

2. Click the item with the color you want to change.

3. Click the new color.

4. Click OK to accept the new screen colors.

Search Disk

Purpose

Searches for ASCII or Hex character strings on a disk. The maximum size of a search string is 32 characters.

To find a string on a disk

1. Select the disk you want to search. Press Ctrl-A, Ctrl-B, or Ctrl-C to select drive A, B, or C.

2. Press F10. From the Disk menu, select Search Disk.

3. Type the string for which you want to search in the Disk Search Service dialog box.

   If you are searching for ASCII characters, type the string of ASCII characters on the ASCII default line. The ASCII search is not case sensitive. The matching hexadecimal values appear on the HEX line.

   To search for HEX values, press Alt-H. Then type the HEX values on the Hex default line. The HEX search is case sensitive. If you type an invalid HEX value, PC Shell beeps. The matching ASCII values appear on the ASCII line.

4. Press End to begin the search. PC Tools displays matching strings located within the disk. If it does not locate any matching strings, a message appears.

5. Select Continue to search for another occurrence after PC Tools finds a string within a disk. Select Edit to edit the sector containing the matching string. Select Show Filename to display file information. When you finish searching the disk, select Cancel to return to the main PC Shell screen.

To find a character string on a disk using a mouse

1. Select the disk you want to search by clicking the drive letters in the upper-left corner of the main PC Shell screen.

2. From the Disk menu, click Search Disk.

3. Follow Steps 3 through 5 of the preceding instructions to begin the search process.

Size/Move Window

PCSHELL

Purpose

Changes the sizes of or moves the active Tree Window and the File List Window.

To size a window

1. Select the window you want to size by using one of these commands:

   • Press Tab. Each time you press Tab, the active window switches back and forth.

   • Press F10. From the Options menu, select Tree/Files Switch. Repeat this procedure to make the active window switch back and forth.

2. Press F10. From the Options menu, select Si Ze/Move Window.

   Alternatively, press **Alt-Space bar**.

3. Select Size from the Window Control dialog box.

4. Use the movement keys to resize the window.

   The upper-left corner of the window remains stationary, but the lower-right corner of the window moves.

5. Press Enter after you size the window.

To size a window using a mouse

1. Move the mouse to either window, and click to make that window active.

2. Move the mouse to the top window border.

3. Press and hold the mouse button. Drag the window to its new location.

4. Release the mouse button.

The upper-left corner of the window remains stationary, but the lower-right corner of the window moves.

To move a window

1. Select the window you want to move by using either of these commands:

   • Press **Tab**. Each time you press **Tab**, you toggle between the two windows to determine which is active.

   • Press **F10**. From the **O**ptions menu, select **T**ree/Files Switch. Repeat the keystroke combination to toggle between the windows.

2. Press **F10**. From the **O**ptions menu, select SiZe/Move Window.

   Alternatively, press **Alt-Space bar**.

3. Select **M**ove from the Window Control dialog box.

4. Use the movement keys to move the window.

   The size of the window does not change when you move it. Only the position of the window on your computer screen changes.

5. Press **Enter** after you size the window.

To move a window using a mouse

1. Move the mouse to either window, and click the window to make it active.

2. From the **Options** menu, click **Size/Move Window**.

3. Move the mouse to the top window border.

Do not position the mouse in the close box, located in the upper-left corner of the window.

4. Press the mouse button and drag the window to its new location.

Status Line

PCSHELL

Purpose

Displays the number of files in the directory. In addition, the Status line shows the total number of bytes that are in the files within the selected directory. The status line also shows the total number of selected files, how many bytes are in those selected files, and the total number of free or unused bytes on the disk.

To view the Status Line

PC Shell always displays the status line on the main PC Shell screen. This line is located directly under the Tree and File List windows.

System Info

PCSHELL

Purpose

Checks and reports on what kind of computer you are using, its configuration, and supplies other useful information.

Notes

The System Information Service dialog box provides the following types of information:

Computer	Reads a ROM/BIOS signature. If your computer is an IBM or compatible, displays name of your

	computer. If it cannot tell what computer you are using, it does not display this line.
BIOS programs are dated	Displays date built-in BIOS (Basic Input/Output System) was last changed. Enter the new date each time you update computer's BIOS.
Operating System	Displays version of DOS used to boot your computer.
Number of logical	Displays number of disk drives connected, including floppy drives, hard disks, RAM disks (electronic disks), and so on.
	The number of logical disk drives is often displayed as A through E (or five drives), even if there are not five drives actually installed on your computer. This number can be controlled also with the LASTDRIVE option in your CONFIG.SYS file.
Logical drive letter range	Displays drive letter names available for drives connected to your computer.
Serial ports	Displays number of serial ports connected to your computer.
Parallel ports	Displays number of parallel ports connected to your computer.
CPU Type	Displays type of processor installed (8088, 80286, and so on) in your computer.
Relative Speed	Displays CPU processing speed of your computer as measured by the original IBM PC running at 4.77 MHz.
Math co-processor present	Reports whether a math co-processor is installed in your computer.

User Programs are loaded at HEX	Displays location where operating system and resident programs are loaded.
Memory used by DOS and resident programs	Displays size of computer's operating system and resident programs. Operating system uses the lowest area of computer memory and user programs are loaded directly after this.
	When the numbers in the memory used by DOS and the Resident Programs section of the System Information Service dialog box are larger, the operating system (and any other resident programs loaded before PC Shell) is using more memory. Less memory, therefore, is available for your other computer programs.
Memory available for user programs	Displays amount of computer memory available for use by your other computer programs.
Total memory reported by DOS	Displays amount of computer memory available in DOS for your use.
PC Shell has found the total memory to be	Displays actual amount of computer memory available. Ignores any memory switch settings in determining how much memory is available in your computer (up to 640K).
	If the "Total memory reported by DOS," and the "PC Shell has found the memory numbers to be" disagree, then the switches in your computer are set wrong, or another

	program, such as a RAM disk or print spooler, has taken some of your computer's memory.
Video Display Type	Reports the type of display adapter your computer uses. PC Shell recognizes CGA, EGA, Mono, VGA, and PGA adapters.
Additional ROM BIOS found at HEX paragraph	Reports whether any expansion boards are plugged into your PC that contain "extensions" to the PC BIOS. If it does not find any expansion boards, it does not display this line.

To display system information

1. Press **F10**. From the **O**ptions menu, select **S**ystem Info.

2. Press **Esc** to return to the main PC Shell screen.

To reset selected files using a mouse

From the **Special** menu, click **System Info**.

Telecommunications

DESKTOP

Purpose

Communicates with other computers via modem. Uses your computer's communications ports to send and receive data to and from your computer.

Notes

Telecommunications can operate in the background, enabling you to transmit and receive data while you are running other applications. Telecommunications also uses scripts so that you can automatically call and log onto another computer.

Components of the Telecommunications screen

The Telecommunications screen contains several parts:

Horizontal Menu Bar	Contains pull-down menus and on-line Help.
Window Border	Designates the active window with a double-line border. If a window is inactive, it is displayed with a single-line border.
Close Box	Located in upper-left corner of window. Used with the mouse to close the window and to exit Telecommunications.
File Name	Displays name of current phone directory. Identifies phone directories by the .TEL file extension.
Telecom- munications Window	Main section of window containing brief information for each entry placed in the phone directory.

Information in the Telecommunications window

COM Port	Displays communications port your computer uses to send information to your modem.
Name	Contains a label assigned to each entry displayed in Telecommuni- cations window. Usually the name of the computer service (Compu- Serve, for example), or the name of someone you send files to on a regular basis.
	To select an entry quickly, type a number to the left of the name.
Number	Displays phone number you want your computer to dial to make a connection with another computer.

If you do not enter a number, Telecommunication asks for the number each time you choose to dial the entry.

Baud

Sets speed at which communication takes place. Baud rate should match the speed of your computer and modem.

Duplex

Determines how computers handle transmitted data. Many systems are full duplex.

PDS

Sets character format used during data transmission.

Improper settings prevent normal communications. If you register for service to a computer information service or receive permission to access another computer system, you are usually issued a password. You should also receive a manual or other documentation describing the PDS, baud, and duplex settings required to connect to the system.

Script file

Contains name of script file used by Telecommunications to perform automatic dialing and logging onto another computer.

Scroll bar

Use with mouse to move or scroll through phone directory entries.

Message bar

Displays messages to assist you with your work in Telecommunications.

To start Telecommunications

From the Desktop main screen, select Telecommunications.

To load an existing phone directory

1. Press F10. From the File menu, select Load.

2. Press **Tab** to select the name of the phone directory you want to use in the File Load dialog box.

3. Press **Alt-L** to select **L**oad.

To load a new phone directory

1. Press **F10**. From the **F**ile menu, select **L**oad.

2. Type the name of a new phone directory (use the .TEL extension) in the File Load dialog box.

3. Press **Alt-N** to select **N**ew.

To save a phone directory

1. Press **F10**. From the **F**ile menu, select **S**ave.

2. Press **Alt-S** to **S**ave the file displayed in the Send File to Disk dialog box.

To change phone directory parameters

1. Press **Tab** to select the line you want to edit.

2. Press **F10**. From the **E**dit menu, select **E**dit Entry.

3. Press **Tab** to select any of these communications parameters:

Name
Text Box

Types the name of the person, company, or computer service you are calling. The entry can contain up to 50 characters.

Phone
Number
Text Box

Types the phone number, as well as any additional commands used by your modem to dial the phone. Telecommuni-cations disregards spaces, dashes, and parentheses.

This entry can contain up to 50 characters, but only 25 are displayed from the main phone directory screen. You can leave the phone number text box empty if you want to set the communi-cations settings only.

Script File
Text Box

Types the file name and .SCR extension for your script file containing commands for automatic dialing.

Terminal

Determines whether you need the ability to imitate a Teletype terminal.

Port

Selects serial port on your computer to use for communications.

Duplex

Selects type of setting used to transmit data. Selects full or half. Most systems are full duplex. If, during communications, you cannot see what you are typing, change this setting to half. If you see two of each character, change this setting to full.

PDS

Selects Parity, Data-Bits, and Stop-Bits. These settings specify how characters are transferred. Your computer and the computer you are calling must have the same PDS settings. If not, you receive no characters, or nonsensical characters.

The parity, data-bits, and stop-bits are normally set at no parity, eight data-bits, and one stop-bit, respectively. However, you can select any required combination.

Baud

Selects transmission speed. The higher the number, the faster the transmission; however, your modem determines how high the number can be that you select.

Dialing

Selects touch-tone or pulse (rotary) dialing.

End-of-line Processing	Selects how the end of each line is processed. Check the manual that came with your subscription service for the correct setting.
Receive	Selects Add LF (add a line feed), Add CR (add a carriage return), or None.
Send	Selects Send LF (send a line feed), Send CR (send a carriage return), or None.
Flow Control	Selects with None or XON/XOFF. Controls flow of data between two computers with less chance of data loss. Use when one computer needs time to accept a file from the other. Setting must be the same for both computers.

4. Press **Alt-A** to Accept the new settings.

To edit a phone directory

1. Press **F10**. From the Edit menu, select Create New Entry.

2. Press **Tab** to select any of the communications parameters.

3. Press **Alt-A** to Accept the new settings.

To remove a phone directory

1. Press **Tab** to select the line you want to remove.

2. Press **F10**. From the Edit menu, select Remove entry.

To dial automatically another computer

Perform one of the following operations:

- Press **Tab** to select the line that displays the computer you want to call. Next, press **F10**. From the Actions menu, select Dial.

- Type the number displayed to the left of the entry. Press **Enter**.

- Double-click the line that displays the desired computer.

If the line does not display a phone number, a dialog box appears, and you must type the desired phone number. Press **Alt-A** to **A**ccept the phone number.

To manually dial another computer

1. Press **Tab** to select the line that displays the computer you want to call.

2. Press **F10**. From the **A**ctions menu, select **M**anual.

3. Type the required dialing sequence in the Telecommunications window.

To hang up the phone

Press **F10**. From the **A**ctions menu, select **H**ang Up Phone.

To end a transfer

Press **F10**. From the **A**ctions menu, select End **T**ransfer.

To receive an ASCII file

1. Press **F10**. From the **R**eceive menu, select **A**SCII.

   Alternatively, press **F6**.

2. Type the name of the file you want to receive.

3. Select **S**ave to begin receiving the file.

4. Select End **T**ransfer after you receive the file.

To receive an XMODEM file

1. Press **F10**. From the **R**eceive menu, select **X**MODEM.

   Alternatively, press **F7**.

2. Type the name of the file you want to receive.

3. Select **S**ave to begin receiving the file.

4. Select End **T**ransfer after you receive the file.

To send an ASCII file

1. Press **F10**. From the Send menu, select **A**SCII.

   Alternatively, press **F4**.

2. Press **Tab** to select the file you want to send.

3. Press **Alt-L** to select **L**oad.

To send an XMODEM file

1. Press **F10**. From the Send menu, select **X**MODEM.

   Alternatively, press **F5**.

2. Press **Tab** to select the file you want to send.

3. Press **Alt-L** to select **L**oad.

Tree/Files Switch

PCSHELL

Purpose

Toggles between the File List window and the Tree List window. By switching between these two windows, you make one active, and you then can make selections.

Note

You select directories in the Tree List window and you select files in the File List window.

To switch between Tree and File List windows

Perform one of these procedures:

- Press **Tab**. Each time you press **Tab**, the active window switches back and forth between Tree and File List.

- Press **F10**. From the **O**ptions menu, select **T**ree/Files Switch. Repeat this keystroke combination to toggle between active windows.

To switch windows using a mouse

Move the mouse to the other window, and click once to make the window active.

Two List Display

PCSHELL

Purpose

Displays a second set of Tree and File List windows. You can open another directory or drive in the second set of windows. Useful when copying, moving, or comparing files from one drive to another, or from one directory to another.

To switch to a two list display

1. Press **Ins**.

   Alternatively, press **F10**. From the **O**ptions menu, select **TW**o List Display.

2. Select a second directory or drive in either of the two Tree List windows.

Shortcut: Press **Ctrl-Alt-A** or **Ctrl-Alt-B** to display the second list and contents of the selected drive.

To switch to a two list display using a mouse

1. From the **O**ptions menu, click **Two List Display**.

2. Click the new drive or directory in either of the two Tree List windows.

Use the **S**ave Configuration command located in the **O**ptions menu to save the two-list display settings for your next PC Shell session.

Undelete

PCSHELL

Purpose

Recovers files that you deleted.

Notes

You can delete more than one file at a time. This is useful if you have deleted an entire disk with the DOS DEL *.* command.

You also can recover removed subdirectories by using Undelete.

If you delete a file accidentally, do not use the disk again until you run Undelete. DOS may overwrite another file on the disk, therefore destroying or losing your data.

There are three methods to recover deleted files or subdirectories.

• Delete Tracking Method

• Standard DOS Method

• Create a File Method

If you plan to undelete a file from a floppy disk, use the Copy Disk command to create a copy of the disk. Use the copied disk to recover your deleted file. After you recover the file, you can then copy the file back to the original disk. You must use Disk Copy—not File Copy—to copy the deleted file to the second disk.

To use the Delete Tracking Method

The method of undeleting a file works by installing a small resident program with MIRROR. Each time you turn on your computer, the Delete Tracking option in your AUTOEXEC.BAT file keeps track of all files you delete. This information is kept in a file called PCTRACKR.DEL. If you need to run undelete, PC Shell

uses the information in the file to locate the deleted files'
address information. This method of undeleting a file
can recover fragmented files if the data has not been
overwritten, and if you have not installed the Mirror
program.

To use the Standard DOS Method

This method of undeleting a file works by renaming a
deleted file. When DOS deletes a file, it really is not
erased, but rather the first character of a file is changed
to a question mark (?). If your October report was saved
in a file called OCTOBER.RPT, for example, when you
delete the file, DOS changes the name of the file to
?CTOBER.RPT. DOS does not erase the contents of the
file. Instead, the question mark tells DOS to write over
those sectors that hold the OCTOBER.RPT data.

With the standard DOS method of undeleting a file, PC
Shell looks for any deleted files (those files with a
question mark for its first character), and then enables
you to change the first character from a question mark to
a standard file character. After you change the first
character, you can access and use the file.

If you have not installed MIRROR, use this method to
undelete files.

To use the Create File Method

If the File Tracking or Standard DOS method of
undeleting a file does not work, you still have one last
chance to recover your data by creating a file, and then
adding clusters to it. Use this method only if you are
reasonably sure the information is still on the disk, but
that you cannot recover it with Standard DOS or File
Tracking undeletion.

Use this method of recovering data for ASCII text files
only. You usually cannot piece together binary files
because it is too difficult to establish which clusters to
add.

Data Recovery

There are two methods of recovery when running
undelete: automatic and manual. If a file is listed in the

Undelete Service dialog box with a @ character next to the file name, PC Tools can undelete that file automatically.

If you are using the Delete Tracking method, and if there is no @ character after the file name, you cannot use the Delete Tracking method to undelete a file. If an asterisk (*) appears next to the file name, PC Tools cannot delete that file automatically. This character indicates that some of the clusters are available, but not all of them.

If neither the ? nor * character is displayed next to a file name, the file cannot be undeleted.

If you can undelete a file with the Automatic method, the Undelete Service dialog box informs you that the file has been recovered. If you cannot undelete the file with the Automatic method, the Undelete Service dialog box prompts you to use the manual method.

Manual data recovery commands

If you must use the manual method to recover a deleted file, these commands are available:

PgUp	Moves display to previous quarter sector
PgDn	Moves display to next quarter sector
Home	Moves to beginning of cluster
End	Moves to end of cluster

Manual file undeletion commands

These commands are available for manual file undeletion:

Add	Adds cluster to file and moves to next cluster
S Kip	Skips to next cluster, not adding current cluster to the file
Save	Saves clusters to file being undeleted

SRch   Displays Undelete Service dialog
                box and searches for additional
                clusters that may contain
                information on file to undelete.

SeL   Enters and selects new cluster.
                Select Continue to select new
                cluster and return to Undelete
                Service dialog box, or select EXit
                to stop cluster move.

Edit   Reorders added clusters to a
                deleted file. Moves or removes
                added clusters. After the move or
                remove is completed, select OK to
                continue with the undeletion.

                To move cluster during edit,
                highlight cluster you want to move
                with left- or right-arrow key or
                with mouse. Select Move and move
                highlighted cluster to new position
                in list. Select OK when cluster is
                relocated.

                To remove cluster during edit,
                highlight cluster you want to
                remove with left- or right-arrow
                key or mouse. Select Remove.
                Cluster is removed from the list.

EXit   Returns to Undelete Service dialog
                box. Select Continue to return to
                the main PC Shell screen.

PC Tools displays the number of clusters that must be
added to complete the file. It also displays the current
number of clusters being added, as well as the cluster
and sector number.

Use the Add command if the displayed cluster seems to
be a part of the deleted file. The cluster is then added to
the file being recovered, and Undelete jumps to the next
cluster.

Use the SKip command to ignore the current cluster so
that PC Tools does not add it to the file it is recovering.
Undelete jumps to the next cluster.

You can organize the clusters better if you look at the text at the bottom of the current cluster. Suppose that you see the beginning of a sentence, *Learning about word pro*, for example. If the next cluster does not start with the characters *cessors* (the rest of the word *processors*), this is the wrong cluster.

Select Save to rebuild the file after you select all the correct clusters.

Try using the file after it is recovered. If you selected incorrect clusters, the file is not the same as the original file. To reorganize the file, try deleting it again, and then undelete it, choosing different clusters.

To undelete a file using Delete Tracking method

1. Press **Tab** to select the Tree List window. Select the directory containing the file you want to undelete in the Tree List window. Use the movement keys to highlight the directory.

2. Press **F10**. From the Special menu, select Undelete.

3. Select Continue to confirm that the selected drive and subdirectory contain the file to undelete.

4. Select File to undelete a file.

5. Select Del Track in the Undelete Service dialog box.

6. Press the **down arrow** to select a file to undelete.

7. Select Go by pressing **Alt-G**.

To undelete a file using Standard DOS method

1. Press **Tab** to select the Tree List window. Select the directory containing the file you want to undelete in the Tree List window. Use the movement keys to highlight the directory.

2. Press **F10**. From the Special menu, select Undelete.

3. Select Continue to confirm that the selected drive and subdirectory contain the file to undelete.

4. Select File to undelete a file.

5. Select Dos Dir in the Undelete Service dialog box.

6. Press the **down arrow** to select a file to undelete.

7. Select **G**o by pressing **Alt-G**.

8. Type the first letter of the file name you want to undelete.

9. Press **Enter** to select **U**ndelete.

10. Select **A**utomatic if the @ character appears next to the file name. Alternatively, select **M**anual if the @ character does not appear next to the file name.

11. Select **C**ontinue to return to the main PC Shell screen.

To undelete a file using the Create File method

1. Press **Tab** to select the Tree List window. Select the directory containing the file you want to undelete in the Tree List window. Use the movement keys to highlight the directory.

2. Press **F10**. From the **S**pecial menu, select **U**ndelete.

3. Select **C**ontinue to confirm that the selected drive and subdirectory contain the files to undelete.

4. Select **C**reate to undelete a file.

5. Type the name and extension of the file you are creating. Press **Alt-R** to create the new file.

6. Select **A**dd to choose the desired clusters.

7. Select **S**ave, and then select E**X**it to return to the main PC Shell screen.

To undelete a file using a mouse

1. Select the directory containing the file you want to undelete by clicking it in the Tree List window.

2. From the **Special** menu, click **Undelete**.

3. Click **Continue** to confirm that the selected drive and subdirectory contain the file you want to undelete.

4. Click **File** to undelete a file.

5. Click **Dos Dir** in the Undelete Service dialog box.

6. Click the file you want to undelete.

7. Click Go.

8. Type the first letter of the file name you want to undelete.

9. Click Enter to select Undelete.

10. Click Automatic if the @ character appears next to the file name. Click Manual if the @ character does not appear next to the file name.

11. Click Continue to return to the main PC Shell screen.

Utilities

DESKTOP

Purpose

Provides a hotkey selection choice, an ASCII table, a system menu/window colors selection, and a program to unload PC Tools Desktop from your computer's memory.

To change the Hotkey selection

1. Select Hotkey Selection from the Utilities menu.

2. Select Desk Hotkey in the dialog box.

3. Press the key combinations you want.

If you want to change the hotkey, it is best to use the Ctrl or Shift key, in combination with the function keys.

To use the ASCII table

1. From the Utilities menu, select ASCII-Table.

2. Press the character you want to find in the table.

To change the system menu/window colors

1. Select System Menu/Window Colors from the Utilities menu.

2. Select any of the options in the Color Selection dialog box.

3. Select any of the color options.

4. Press Esc to close the dialog box.

To unload PC Tools Desktop

1. Select the Utilities menu.

2. Press Tab to select Unload PC Tools Desktop and press Enter.

Verify Disk

PCSHELL

Purpose

Confirms that DOS can read all the data on your disk. Checks the data in files, directories, and unused space on the disk.

Notes

PC Shell flags any bad sectors on the disk that have not been marked previously, and displays the sector number containing the error, as well as the location of the bad sector. PC Shell reports the sector's location as a part of the DOS system area, part of an existing file, or as space available for use.

If the bad sector was available for use, PC Shell now marks it as a bad sector, and prevents DOS from using the bad sector to store one of your files.

If PC Shell locates a bad sector being used by a file or subdirectory, a message appears advising you to run the Compress Surface Scan option. This program attempts to move the data to a safe area elsewhere on the disk.

You cannot use Verify Disk on unformatted disks because they contain no information; it works with formatted DOS disks only.

You cannot verify a copy-protected disk. Make sure that
you remove the copy protection of the disk. On a 5 1/4-
inch disk, remove the tiny label over the slot on the right
side of the disk; on a 3 1/2-inch disk, move the slot to
the non-copy-protected position before running Verify
Disk.

To verify a disk

1. Select the disk you want to search. Press **Ctrl-A**,
   Ctrl-B, or **Ctrl-C** to select drive A, B, or C.

2. Press **F10**. From the **D**isk menu, select **V**erify.

3. Press **Enter** to Verify the selected disk.

4. Press **Enter** to select E**X**it and to return to the main
   PC Shell screen.

To verify a disk using a mouse

1. Select the disk you want to search by clicking the
   drive letters in the upper-left corner of the main PC
   Shell screen.

2. From the **D**isk menu, click **Verify Disk**.

3. Click **Verify**

4. Click **E**xit to return to the main PC Shell screen.

Verify File

PCSHELL

Purpose

Reads all sectors in any particular file to make sure DOS
can read the entire file without any errors. The Verify
command can check a single file or any number of files.

To verify a file

1. Select the file you want to verify by using the
   movement keys to highlight the file name. Press
   Enter.

2. Press **F10**. From the **F**ile menu, select **V**erify.

3. The File Verify Service dialog box displays the current file name and extension. As Verify works its way through the file, the sector number of the selected file changes. If Verify does not discover any errors, a message appears within the File Verify Service dialog box stating that the file is okay. If you selected more than one file, Verify continues through the list of selected files.

4. Select E**X**it by pressing **Enter** to exit the File Verify Service dialog box, and to return to the main PC Shell screen.

If Verify discovers an error within a file, the File Verify Service dialog box displays the logical sector that contains the error. To repair the sector, select View/Edit from the File Verify Service dialog box. Then select **S**ave to rewrite the corrected sector information back onto your disk. This procedure should make the sector readable, but some information rewritten on the sector may be invalid. This procedure recovers as much of your data as possible.

To verify a file using a mouse

1. Select the file to verify by clicking it.

2. From the **File** menu, click **Verify**.

3. Click **Exit** after PC Shell verifies the file.

View

PCSHELL

Purpose

Enables you to view any file. If you are viewing a dBASE or Lotus 1-2-3 file, View displays the file in a database or spreadsheet format.

Notes

If the file you are viewing is not a Lotus 1-2-3 or dBASE file, PC Shell displays it in standard ASCII/Hex format. To edit a file, use Hex Edit.

Launch automatically runs dBASE or Lotus, and then loads and displays the file just as if you exited PC Shell, and started Lotus or dBASE as usual. Launch works much faster.

To run Lotus or dBASE with the Launch command in View, the Applications menu of PC Shell must display these applications. If you used PC Setup to install PC Shell, and Lotus 1-2-3 or dBASE was on your disk, it should be installed automatically on your applications menu.

To view a file

1. Select the file to view.

2. Press **F10**. From the **F**ile menu, select **V**iew.

To view a Lotus 1-2-3 file

1. Select the Lotus 1-2-3 file to view.

2. Press **F10**. From the **F**ile menu, select **V**iew.

3. Use any of these commands to move through the Lotus 1-2-3 file:

Key	*Action*
Right arrow	Moves one column to the right
Left arrow	Moves one column to the left
Up arrow	Moves up one line
Down arrow	Moves down one line
Home	Goes to beginning of worksheet
End	Goes to end of worksheet
PgUp	Scrolls up one window
PgDn	Scrolls down one window
Ctrl-Left arrow	Scrolls one window to the left

Ctrl-Right arrow	Scrolls one window to the right
L	Launches Lotus and loads the selected file
N	Goes to the next file

To run Lotus from View

1. Select the Lotus 1-2-3 file to view.

2. Press **F10**. From the **F**ile menu, select **V**iew.

3. Select **L**aunch to run Lotus 1-2-3 automatically.

To view a dBASE file

1. Select the dBASE file to view.

2. Press **F10**. From the **F**ile menu, select **V**iew.

3. Use any of these scroll commands to move through the file:

Key	*Function*
F	Toggles between first and last record
G	Goes to specified record
P	Goes to prior record
X	Goes to next record
S	Searches for character string
R	Repeats search
I	Views database statistics
L	Launches dBASE and load selected file
N	Goes to next file

To run dBASE from View

1. Select the dBASE file to view.

2. Press **F10**. From the **F**ile menu, select **V**iew.

3. Select **L**aunch to run dBASE automatically.

View/Edit Disk

PCSHELL

Purpose

Views inside any sector on the disk. The sector can be part of any DOS file. After viewing the sector, you can edit or change it.

Notes

Before making any changes to any sector of the disk with this command, you should have a working knowledge and understanding of ASCII and hexadecimal values and sector bytes. Making improper changes to your files with the View/Edit Disk command can cause your programs to be inoperable.

The following keys are available in the View/Edit Disk Service dialog box:

Home	Moves to first sector on disk
End	Moves to last sector on disk
PgUp	Repositions display to previous half-sector on disk
PgDn	Repositions display to next half-sector on disk
Esc	Exits to main PC Shell screen
F5	Saves changes made during editing process
F6	Cancels changes made during editing process
F8	Toggles between HEX and ASCII display

To view a disk

1. Select the disk to view. Press **Ctrl-A**, **Ctrl-B**, or **Ctrl-C** to select drive A, B, or C.

2. Press **F10**. From the **D**isk menu, select View/**E**dit Disk.

3. Select Cancel to return to the main PC Shell screen.

To edit a disk

These commands are available when working in the
Disk View/Edit Service dialog box:

Edit	Makes changes to sector on disk.
Name	Displays file name where sector goes.
Cancel	Returns you to main PC Shell menu.
	You also can press Esc to return to the main screen.
Change Sector	Displays special dialog box offering six move-to options. You can change the sector to one of the following:

Boot Sector moves to first byte of disk Boot Record.

First FAT Sector moves to first byte of File Allocation Table on disk.

First Root DIR Sector moves to first byte of Root Directory on disk.

First Data Sector moves to first byte of first Data Sector on disk.

Change Cluster # enters cluster number (2-83647) to move to specific cluster on disk.

Change Sector # enters sector number to move to specific sector on disk.

After you make a selection from this special dialog box, select Continue to complete the Change Sector process, or select EXit to return to the main PC Shell screen.

On most hard disks, the sector size is a multiple of 512 bytes. The View/Edit command displays 256 bytes, or a half sector, on-screen.

To read the Sector Edit service screen

This screen displays each of the 512 bytes of the sector, starting with number 0 and ending with number 511. (These are hexadecimal numbers running from 0000 to 01FF.) Each line of the display shows 16 bytes. These 16 bytes also display in ASCII values in the right column on-screen. The first line starts at byte 0, and runs through byte 15; the next line starts at byte 16, and runs through byte 31, and so on.

The displacement number, located in the far left column, indicates how many bytes each line is into the sector. The numbers in the parentheses (listed beside the displacement numbers on the left side of the screen) are the same numbers, but they are displayed in hexadecimal.

The middle column displays each line within the sector.

Some of the ASCII values may appear unreadable, or may appear to be displayed in strange symbols. This is because those bytes may be program or data values; they were never meant to be displayed as text.

To edit a sector on the disk

1. Select the disk to edit. Press **Ctrl-A**, **Ctrl-B**, or **Ctrl-C** to select drive A, B, or C.

2. Press **F10**. From the **D**isk menu, select View/**E**dit Disk.

3. Select **E**dit from the Disk View/Edit Service dialog box.

4. Use the movement keys to move the cursor to the first byte.

5. Type the new hexadecimal value.

   You can make changes in the ASCII column by pressing **F8**.

6. Select **S**ave to write the edited changes to your disk. Alternatively, press **F5**. You are returned to the main PC Shell menu.

To edit a sector on the disk using a mouse

1. Select the disk you want to edit by clicking the drive letters that appear in the upper left of the main PC Shell screen.

2. From the Disk menu, click View/Edit.

3. Click Edit in the Disk View/Edit Service dialog box.

4. Use the scroll bars on the right side of the screen to scroll through the disk sectors to the first byte you want to edit.

5. Type the new hexadecimal value.

6. Click Save to write the edited changes to your disk, and to return to the main PC Shell menu.

Zoom

PCSHELL

Purpose

Automatically resizes the active File and Tree List windows.

To use Zoom

1. Press Tab to select the window.

2. Press Zoom to expand the window.

3. Press Zoom to return the window to its previous size.

Index

que®

11711 N. College Avenue, P.O. Box 90, Carmel, IN 46032
(800) 428-5331 · (317) 573-2510 · FAX: 317-573-2583

1-2-3 Database Techniques	$22.95	Style Sheets for Business Documents	$39.95
1-2-3 for Business, 2nd Edition	$22.95	Style Sheets for Newsletters	$39.95
1-2-3 Macro Library, 2rfd Edition	$21.95	Style Sheets for Technical Documents	$39.95
1-2-3 QueCards	$21.95	The AutoDesk File	$24.95
1-2-3 QuickStart	$21.95	The Big Mac Book	$27.95
1-2-3 Release 2.2 Quick Reference	$7.95	Turbo C Programming	$22.95
1-2-3 Release 2.2 QuickStart	$21.95	Turbo Pascal Advanced Techniques	$22.95
1-2-3 Release 3 Business Applications	$39.95	Turbo Pascal Programmer's Toolkit	$39.95
1-2-3 Release 3 Quick Reference	$7.95	Turbo Pascal Quick Reference	$7.95
1-2-3 Release 3 QuickStart	$21.95	Understanding UNIX, 2nd Edition	$21.95
1-2-3 Release 3 Workbook and Disk	$29.95	Upgrading and Repairing PCs	$27.95
1-2-3 Tips, Tricks, and Traps, 2nd Edition	$21.95	Upgrading to 1-2-3 Release 3	$14.95
1-2-3 Tips, Tricks, and Traps, 3rd Edition	$22.95	Using 1-2-3 Release 2.2, Special Edition	$24.95
AppleWorks QuickStart	$19.95	Using 1-2-3 Release 3	$24.95
Assembly Language Quick Reference	$7.95	Using 1-2-3, Special Edition	$24.95
AutoCAD Advanced Techniques	$34.95	Using 1-2-3 Workbook and Disk, 2nd Edition	$29.95
AutoCAD for Architects and Engineers	$29.95	Using AppleWorks, 2nd Edition	$21.95
AutoCAD Quick Reference	$7.95	Using Assembly Language	$24.95
AutoCAD Reference Guide	$11.95	Using AutoCAD	$29.95
C Programmer's Toolkit	$39.95	Using Clipper	$24.95
C Programming Guide, 3rd Edition	$24.95	Using Computers in Business	$24.95
C Quick Reference	$7.95	Using DacEasy	$21.95
CAD and Desktop Publishing Guide	$24.95	Using DataEase	$22.95
Customizing AutoCAD, 2nd Edition	$27.95	Using dBASE Mac	$19.95
dBASE III Plus Applications Library	$21.95	Using DisplayWrite 4, 2nd Edition	$19.95
dBASE III Plus Handbook, 2nd Edition	$22.95	Using Dollars and Sense: IBM Version, 2nd Edition	$19.95
dBASE III Plus Tips, Tricks, and Traps	$21.95	Using Dollars and Sense	$19.95
dBASE III Plus Workbook and Disk	$29.95	Using DOS	$22.95
dBASE IV Applications Library	$39.95	Using Enable/OA	$23.95
dBASE IV Handbook, 3rd Edition	$23.95	Using Excel	$21.95
dBASE IV Programming Techniques	$24.95	Using Excel: IBM Version	$24.95
dBASE IV QueCards	$21.95	Using Framework III	$26.95
dBASE IV Quick Reference	$7.95	Using FullWrite Professional	$21.95
dBASE IV QuickStart	$19.95	Using Generic CADD	$24.95
dBASE IV Tips, Tricks, and Traps, 2nd Edition	$21.95	Using Harvard Graphics	$24.95
dBASE IV Workbook and Disk	$29.95	Using Harvard Project Manager	$24.95
dBXL and QuickSilver Programming	$24.95	Using HyperCard	$24.95
Desktop Manager	$99.95	Using Lotus Magellan	$21.95
DisplayWrite QuickStart	$19.95	Using Managing Your Money, 2nd Edition	$19.95
DOS & BIOS Functions Quick Reference	$7.95	Using Microsoft Windows	$19.95
DOS Programmer's Reference, 2nd Edition	$27.95	Using Microsoft Word 4: Macintosh Version	$21.95
DOS QueCards	$21.95	Using Microsoft Word 5: IBM Version	$21.95
DOS Tips, Tricks, and Traps	$22.95	Using Microsoft Works	$19.95
DOS Workbook and Disk	$29.95	Using Microsoft Works: IBM Version	$21.95
Excel Business Applications: IBM Version	$39.95	Using MultiMate Advantage, 2nd Edition	$19.95
Excel Quick Reference	$7.95	Using Novell NetWare	$24.95
Excel QuickStart	$19.95	Using OS/2	$23.95
Excel Tips, Tricks, and Traps	$22.95	Using PageMaker: IBM Version, 2nd Edition	$24.95
Hard Disk Quick Reference	$7.95	Using PageMaker: Macintosh Version	$24.95
HyperCard QuickStart	$21.95	Using Paradox 3	$22.95
IBM PS/2 Handbook	$21.95	Using PC DOS, 3rd Edition	$23.95
Inside AutoCAD, 5th Edition	$29.95	Using PFS: First Choice	$22.95
Inside AutoLISP	$29.95	Using PFS: First Publisher	$22.95
Inside AutoSketch	$17.95	Using Professional Write	$19.95
Inside Designer	$21.95	Using Q&A, 2nd Edition	$21.95
Inside TOPS	$21.95	Using Quattro	$21.95
Inside Xerox FormBase	$21.95	Using QuickBASIC4	$19.95
Inside Xerox Presents	$21.95	Using Quicken	$19.95
Inside Xerox Ventura Publisher, 2nd Edition	$29.95	Using Reflex	$19.95
Introduction to Business Software	$14.95	Using Smart	$22.95
Managing Desktop Publishing	$9.95	Using SmartWare II	$24.95
Managing Your Hard Disk, 2nd Edition	$22.95	Using Sprint	$21.95
Microsoft Word 5 Quick Reference	$7.95	Using SuperCalc5, 2nd Edition	$22.95
Microsoft Word 5 Tips, Tricks, and Traps:		Using Symphony, 2nd Edition	$26.95
IBM Version	$21.95	Using Turbo Pascal	$21.95
MS-DOS Quick Reference	$7.95	Using Ventura Publisher, 2nd Edition	$24.95
MS-DOS QuickStart	$21.95	Using Wingz	$21.95
MS-DOS User's Guide, 3rd Edition	$22.95	Using WordPerfect, 3rd Edition	$21.95
Networking Personal Computers, 3rd Edition	$22.95	Using WordPerfect 5	$24.95
Oracle Programmer's Guide	$24.95	Using WordPerfect: Macintosh Version	$19.95
PC Tools Quick Reference	$7.95	Using WordStar, 2nd Edition	$21.95
Power Graphics Programming	$24.95	Ventura Publisher Techniques and Applications	$22.95
Publishing Power with Ventura, 2nd Edition	$27.95	Ventura Publisher Tips, Tricks, and Traps	$24.95
QuickBASIC Advanced Techniques	$21.95	WordPerfect 5 Workbook and Disk	$29.95
QuickBASIC Programmer's Toolkit	$39.95	WordPerfect Macro Library	$21.95
QuickBASIC Quick Reference	$7.95	WordPerfect Power Techniques	$21.95
R:BASE User's Guide, 3rd Edition	$22.95	WordPerfect QueCards	$21.95
Smart Tips, Tricks, and Traps	$24.95	WordPerfect Quick Reference	$7.95
SQL Programmer's Guide	$29.95	WordPerfect QuickStart	$21.95
Stepping Into AutoCAD, 4th Edition	$29.95	WordPerfect Tips, Tricks, and Traps	$21.95